HOUSTON

and

Galveston

FODOR'S TRAVEL PUBLICATIONS

are compiled, researched, and edited by an international team of travel writers, field correspondents, and editors. The series, which now almost covers the globe, was founded by Eugene Fodor in 1936.

OFFICES

New York & London

Houston and Galveston:

Editor: JACQUI RUSSELL
Assistant Editor: STACI CAPOBIANCO
Illustrations: TED BURWELL
Maps: PICTOGRAPH

FODOR'S

HOUSTON

and

GALVESTON

1988

FODOR'S TRAVEL PUBLICATIONS, INC.
New York & London

ISBN 0-679-01524–8
ISBN 0-340-41841–9 (Hodder & Stoughton)

MANUFACTURED IN THE UNITED STATES OF AMERICA
10 9 8 7 6 5 4 3 2 1

CONTENTS

FOREWORD

Houston is one of the fastest-growing cities in the United States, thanks largely to the oil and space industries. Now the nation's fourth largest city, Houston has plenty to offer any visitor—diverse cultural activities, fine hotels and restaurants, exciting sports events, museums, and theaters. Its principal attractions, however, are NASA's LBJ Space Center, home of our major space programs, and the Astrodomain complex housing a theme park, a stadium, and one of the world's largest exhibit areas.

Galveston, meanwhile, is Texas' favorite beach resort, with 32 miles of white-sand beaches and spectacular fishing offshore. For the landlubber, there are history-seeped landmarks, parks and gardens, and entertainment activities for all age groups.

Fodor's Houston & Galveston is designed to help you plan your own trip based on your time, your budget, your energy, your idea of what this trip should be. We have tried to put together the widest possible *range* of activities to offer you *selections* that will be worthwhile, safe, and of good value. The descriptions we provide are designed to help you make your own intelligent choices from our selections.

If you would like to explore other parts of Texas, see *Fodor's Texas,* from which material for this book has been extracted.

While every care has been taken to ensure the accuracy of the information contained in this guide, the publishers cannot accept responsibility for any errors that may appear.

All prices quoted in this guide are based on those available to us at the time of writing. In a world of rapid change, however, the possibility of inaccurate or out-of-date information can never be totally eliminated. We trust, therefore, that you will take prices quoted as indicators only and will double-check to be sure of the latest figures.

Similary, be sure to check all opening times of museums and galleries. We have found that such times are liable to change without notice, and you could easily make a trip only to find a locked door.

When a hotel closes or a restaurant produces a disappointing meal, let us know, and we will investigte the establishment and the complaint. We are always ready to revise our entries for the following year's edition should the facts warrant it.

Send your letters to the editors at Fodor's Travel Publications, 201 East 50th Street, New York, NY 10022. European readers may prefer to write to Fodor's Travel Publications, 9–10 Market Place, London W1N 7AG, England.

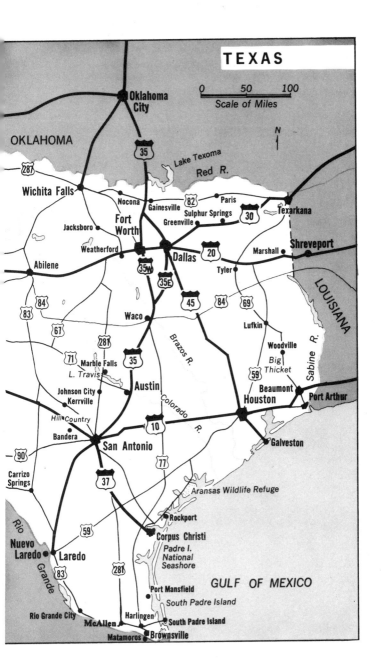

FACTS AT YOUR FINGERTIPS

FACTS AT YOUR FINGERTIPS

FACTS AND FIGURES. Texas, the "Lone Star State" —a sobriquet derived from the state flag—is known for bigness. In a state with an area of more than 2,675,300 square miles, it's easy to understand where the preoccupation with size comes from: Texas is larger than the whole country of France. You will appreciate the long distances if you drive across the state. It is 821 miles (1,321 kilometers) from Texarkana in the northeast to El Paso in the west and 872 miles (1,403 kilometers) from Dalhart in the far north to Brownsville at the southernmost tip. And to get you where you are going, there are more than 70,000 miles of highway in Texas.

But land area is not the only measure of Texas bigness. The state's population topped 16 million in 1986, making Texas number three in the nation. Texas' population is currently growing faster than that of any other state, owing largely to immigration from the Midwest and East Coast states. Today, it is not uncommon to hear a Boston brogue or a Pennsylvania dialect on the streets of Dallas or Fort Worth, alongside the celebrated Texas twang. Fifteen Texas cities have more than 100,000 inhabitants, and Houston with 1.7 million people (three million in the four-county metropolitan area).

Because nineteenth-century Anglo settlement of Texas generally moved from east to west, the most fundamental geographical regions in the state are considered to be East and West Texas. Thick pine forests, flat, lush coastal plains, and grassy, rolling hills are most typical of East Texas; dry, wild regions and the forbidding, empty prairies dominate West Texas. But such a geographic division of the state is imprecise and can pose problems for the uninitiated. In East Texas, the term *West Texas* includes the Panhandle, the northernmost extension of Texas, which resembles the handle of a skillet, whereas in the Panhandle, *West Texas* means the area of desert and mountains west and southwest of Odessa.

For the people of the Panhandle, the top of Texas is simply the Panhandle, a vast land of high plains, endless fields of wheat and cotton, and kaleidoscopic starry vistas at night. Likewise, the term *East Texas* should not include the Central Texas Hill Country, the rather mountainous, arid, and yet water-rich region bounded by Del Rio, San Antonio, Austin, Temple, and San Angelo. *North Texas* indicates the region around and north of the Dallas-Fort Worth metropolitan area. South Texas comprises San Antonio and anything south of there to the Mexican border. Thus, Dallas and Fort Worth are North Texas; Houston, in East Texas; Austin, the capital, in Central Texas; and the port of Corpus Christi, in South Texas. Of course, any native Texan will be glad to argue with you over this breakdown of geographical regions. Go ahead; disputing is a favorite pastime in the state.

Texas is truly a land of contrasts. Mountains more than eight thousand feet dominate the skyline in West Texas, whereas on the plains of the Panhandle's golden spread, you are sometimes lucky to spot a prairie dog mound high enough to break the uniform flatness. In East Texas are some of the thickest, marshiest forests in the nation, but the flat brush country south of San Antonio is almost devoid of high trees—though frequently almost as impenetrable as East Texas forests.

The state possesses great cultural and ethnic diversity too. In addition to the Anglo-Saxon, Hispanic, and black populations, there are long-standing communities of Poles, Czechs, Germans, Lebanese, and other more recent arrivals such as Vietnamese, Cambodians, and Haitians. Each November the Scottish clans of Texas gather in Salado for music and games. The Alabama-Coushatta Indian reservation and village near Livingston draws numerous visitors yearly. In addition, the Cajun-French influence of Louisiana extends across the border into Texas near Orange and Port Arthur.

PLANNING YOUR TRIP. Making reservations for travel and lodging can be tedious, so if you would rather not bother, use a travel agent. The services of a travel agent seldom cost a penny; the agent gets his fee from the hotel or carrier you use. Agents are helpful if you desire a package tour, in which case your pretrip planning would be minimal. If you prefer standardized hotel and motel accommodations, remember that most of the large hostelry chains publish free directories of their members' locations and special qualities.

Auto clubs are a good idea. They are helpful for itineraries, brochures, and emergency services on the road. The American Automobile Association (AAA) is a respected choice. If you live in the United States or Canada, check your local telephone directory for the nearest AAA office; if you are visiting from abroad, call AAA in the first U.S. city you arrive in. If you make your own trip itinerary, be sure the map you use is up to date. For Texas, get the Official Highway Travel Map and other information on places to visit from the state tourist agency.

Make arrangements to board the pets, discontinue newspaper deliveries, and ask a neighbor to keep an eye on your home and pick up the mail. Look into trip insurance (including baggage insurance) and be sure your other policies are up to date. Major credit cards (especially Visa, MasterCard, and American Express) are accepted throughout Texas, so plan on using "plastic" for lodging, gasoline, tickets, and major meals. Consider the safety of carrying at least half of your cash in traveler's checks, and be sure to have on hand sufficient identification (including a photo ID) to avoid undue waiting when cashing them.

TOURIST INFORMATION. The Texas highway department operates tourist bureaus across the state on major highways, plus another bureau in the state capitol in Austin and one in the Judge Roy Bean Visitor Center in Langtry. The bureaus are open daily from 8:00 A.M. to 5:00 P.M. and offer the car traveler valuable brochures on Texas points of interest and copies of the Official Highway Travel Map. Their travel counselors can chart your route, give you comprehensive information about your destination, and suggest things to see and do along the way. Stop by the bureaus or write the State Department of Highways and Public Transportation, Travel and Information Division, P.O. Box 5064, Austin 78763; (512) 836–8640. You can write to request their two publications; the *Texas Travel Handbook,* which includes detailed information on most Texas cities and towns as well as lakes, state and federal parks, hunting and fishing, wildlife, and flowers, and *Texas, The Friendship State,* a book featuring color photographs of various areas in Texas.

Caution: The U.S. Health Department warns that an aggressive, dangerous mosquito, called the Asian tiger mosquito, has been discovered in Texas and other parts of the south. Asian tigers can be efficient transmitters of numerous human diseases, including dengue fever and several forms of encephalitis, which can be fatal. Although none of the Asian tigers in this area have been found to be carrying the diseases, visitors should take precautions against mosquito bites by wearing protective clothing and using insect repellents liberally. Consult with the convention and visitors bureaus in the areas you intend to visit for updated information.

TIPS FOR BRITISH VISITORS. Passports. You will need a valid, 10-year passport and a U.S. visa. You should get your visa either from your travel agent or direct from the United States Embassy, Visa and Immigration Department, 5 Upper Grosvenor St., London W1A 2JB (01–499 3443). Allow *at least* 28 days for your visa to be sent to you if you are applying by post. Visas applied for in person are processed the same day.

No vaccinations are required.

Customs. If you are over 21 you may import into the U.S.: 200 cigarettes or 50 cigars or three pounds of tobacco (a combination of proportionate parts is permitted), one quart of alcohol, and duty-free gifts up to a value of $100. Alcohol and cigarettes may *not* be included in this allowance but 100 cigars may be included.

You may *not* import meat or meat products, seeds, plants, fruits, etc. Avoid narcotics like the plague.

Returning to the U.K.: Except those under 17 years, you may import into the U.K. the following items: 200 cigarettes or 50 cigars or 250 gr. of tobacco, and two liters of still table wine plus one liter of alcoholic drink over 22° proof or two liters under 22° proof (e.g., fortified or sparkling wine) or a further two liters of still table wine, and 50 gr. of perfume and a quarter liter of toilet water. Other articles up to a value of £32 may also be imported along with no more than 50 liters of beer.

Insurance. We cannot recommend too strongly that you insure yourself to cover all health and motoring mishaps. *Europ Assistance,* 252 High St., Croydon, Surrey CRO 1NF (01–680 1234) offers an excellent service, all the more valuable when you consider the possible costs of health care in the U.S.

The *Association of British Insurers,* Aldermary House, Queen St., London EC4N 1TT (01–248 4477) will give comprehensive advice on all aspects of vacation insurance.

Air Fares. We suggest that you explore the current scene for the latest on air fares, including the ever-popular *Virgin Atlantic Airways*. Houston is the hub for *Continental Airlines,* which usually has cut-rate fares for a limited number of seats on flights during off-peak times. Check the APEX fares (at press time, the round-trip on an APEX ticket cost around £354) and other money-saving fares offered by the various major airlines. Another good place to find low-cost fares is in the small ads of the Sunday newspapers, and some magazines, such at *Time Out.* These fares are fiendishly difficult to come across so try and book as early as possible. If you don't fancy doing it all on your own then go to your local travel agent for expert advice.

 WHEN TO GO. Because of long summers and moderate winters in much of the state, the month of your visit really depends on when you *can* go. Outdoor activities that flourish during the spring and long summer include boating, sailing, cycling, golf, tennis, swimming—the list is almost endless. Of course, Texas is not famous for its winter sports—unless you consider hunting, fishing, and January golfing and picnicking as part of a winter-sports regimen. If weather is the determining factor for your trip, however, be advised that from the first of July to mid-September, the weather is *hot* across the whole state and that December through February can be quite cold in the northern half of Texas. If we consider the entire state and all the climatic zones, the best months for touring it are probably April to mid-July and October. But whatever time of year you visit, you are sure to find the sun, and definitely the fun, during your stay.

 CLIMATE. Texas could be called the land of the six-month summer, May through October. In fact, the summers might be even longer were it not for the occasional early and late cold snaps that roll down from the Great Plains states in the north. Springtime is March and April, and autumn hurries by from October to December. Mid-December to the end of February is usually all there is of winter, but even that season is temperate in the southeastern part of the state.

Texas has a continental climate, with the corresponding seasonal extremes in temperature, but the relatively low latitude and the adjacent Gulf of Mexico tend to moderate extremes over much of the state. Draw an imaginary line from Laredo, on the Mexican border, to Waco and then to Marshall, near the Louisiana line: The area southeast of the line has warm to hot, humid summer days and nights, fair springs and falls, and very moderate winters (plenty of sunny January days for golfing and picnicking).

PACKING. The easiest way to accomplish this task is to make a list for each member of the family, then check off each item as you pack it. Remember to keep accessible items you will need for having fun. Pack the film and cameras, the suntan lotion and insect repellent, toilet articles, writing supplies, swimwear, hiking shoes, sun hats, radios, maps, your guidebook, and your vacation reading material in a backpack, a kit bag, or a large purse where you can get at items quickly and easily. If you wear glasses or contact lenses, do not forget to carry spares. If you fly, be careful with your film. No matter what airport security guards may say to the contrary, the X-ray machines at the boarding gate frequently destroy photographic film; ask for a hand inspection.

Make sure everyone has the appropriate footwear for walking. Sturdy leather shoes or boots for the countryside and tennis or jogging shoes for urban asphalt are good choices. You might consider putting all the rain gear in one place. If a downpour strikes, you won't have to hunt everywhere for protection.

Do not take too many clothes. Nothing is more tiresome on a vacation trip than lugging around lots of heavy luggage or trying to find room in an overstuffed car trunk for things purchased on the road.

For most of the year and for most people, the heat, not the cold, will be more of a factor in planning what to wear. From March to October, the tendency is toward warm to hot days and warm, humid nights.

For dressy evenings in Houston, take along your basic cocktail or evening wear. Men will need ties and jackets for some big-city restaurants and clubs, but casual dress is the rule in most places. For sightseeing in the cities in summer, jeans or khaki slacks, shorts, sandals, and T-shirts are fine.

WHAT WILL IT COST? Of course, this is *the* crucial question for most of us. Gasoline and other transportation expenses are somewhat determined by your style of traveling, but they are far more subject to your destination's distance from home and the vagaries of transportation costs. Lodging and food costs, however, depend more on you, your way of doing things, and your tastes. Two people can tour comfortably in Texas for about $130 a day (not counting gasoline or other transport costs), as you can see in the table below.

Typical Daily Expenses for Two People

Room at moderate hotel or motel, including tax	$58
Breakfast at restaurant, including tip	10
Lunch at inexpensive diner, including tip	12
Drinks, dinner with beer or wine, and tip at moderate restaurant	25
Miscellaneous admissions, tour fees, movie tickets, small purchases	25
	$130

Such is a typical cost breakdown for a very comfortable trip: spacious room with TV (but no room service) and not much stinting on meals and incidental drinks and purchases. But in each of these categories you can cut cost corners and free up money for those fun miscellaneous expenses and shopping. Take lodging, for instance. There are several budget motel chains that furnish the same amenities as their more famous competitors but who do so with much less panache. The *Motel 6* chain is one frequently found in Texas. A simple, clean room for two costs under $30 a night, including tax. What do you give up? Well, there is no color TV; maybe there is only a shower instead of a shower-bath; you have to pay a quarter for ice; there is no restaurant attached. All in all, though, you definitely get your money's worth. Two more lodging suggestions are to look for reduced rates in urban hotels on the weekends, when visiting businessmen depart, and to search out motels on the old highway thoroughfares.

As for meals, why not try picnicking once a day and switching to pastries and coffee for breakfast? A portable ice cooler packed with drinks, some sandwich supplies, and a good Thermos can really dent those lunch bills. And a leisurely luncheon in a city or roadside park can be more relaxing than sitting in a busy restaurant. Just make sure to keep your picnic kit accessible in the trunk.

 HINTS TO THE MOTORIST. Because of the fine highways, a wide variety of landscape, and limited rail and bus routes, traveling by motor car is definitely the best way to see Texas.

Although sometimes you may doubt it, Texas observes the national 55-mph (89-kph) speed limit (except, of course, where otherwise indicated). A large anti-55-mph lobby exists in the state, because there are such long distances between the cities. Remember, it is almost 1,000 km. from Houston to Amarillo and more than 1,200 from Houston to El Paso. But the lobby won't help you if you exceed the limit and are stopped by a Texas Department of Public Safety officer. Keep to 55 mph unless lowers speeds are posted. Traffic fatalities have decreased since the nationwide speed limit was instituted.

Lower speed limits are enforced in communities. Watch for signs saying "Speed Zone Ahead" and be prepared to decelerate. Keep alert when driving on weekdays during the school year (August-June); school zones are usually marked with flashing yellow lights and permit only very low speeds. And if you find yourself behind a loading or unloading schoolbus, don't pass or overtake it—it's against the law. Of course, you will encounter few speed zones and schoolbuses on interstate highways and urban expressways.

Before leaving home, have your regular mechanic thoroughly check your car. It might be wise to join an auto club that renders emergency and repair services on the road, or to investigate your auto insurance to see if you are covered for towing and emergency charges. While you are doing that, make sure your insurance policy is in force and take proof of that fact with you.

If you need repairs en route, look for a garage displaying the National Institute for Automotive Service Excellence (NIASE) seal. You may need to check the Yellow Pages of the local telephone directory for auto-parts stores that are open 24 hours a day; quite a few cities have them. But if it is Sunday, you're far from a metropolitan area, and you need that fuel pump or special fan belt for your disabled car, your chances for fast service are slim. To avoid such a scenario, carry some emergency parts and tools in the trunk of your car, along with the jack, the spare tire, and your jumper cables.

Locating gasoline is rarely a problem. If gas stops are few and far-between on a U.S. or a Texas state highway, road signs will indicate the distance to the next service station.

Texas maintains a splendid system of interstate, U.S., and state highways, with an aggregate length of more than 70,000 miles. You will find that your pleasure and knowledge of the land will be increased if you drive some of the many farm-to-market and ranch roads that crisscross major routes. Most of these secondary roads are comparable to regular two-lane, shouldered highways in other states. So if you have the time, be adventurous. Take a few of these not-so-well-traveled roads. For a detailed map of all Texas highways and roads, pick up the Official Highway Travel Map from one of the Texas tourist bureaus. "F.M." means "Farm-to-Market Road," and "R.M." means "Ranch-to-Market Road."

TRAILERS

Towed vehicles or trailers more than 55 ft. (16.8 m.) long or 8 ft. (2.44 m.) wide require special permits in Texas. The permits are good for single trips not exceeding 5 days. The $10 fee is payable by cashier's check, money order, Mastercard, Visa, and you must supply the license number, make, model, and weight of the trailer, plus the license and engine numbers of the towing vehicle. The permits are available from any State Department of Highways and Public Transportation district office and from the Texas tourist bureaus. For more information or to order permits by phone call the Central Permit Office in Austin (800) 227–6839.

 WHAT TO DO WITH THE PETS. Will you take your pet dog or cat on the trip? More and more motels accept them now. Check before you register. If this is your first voyage with your pet, accustom the animal to car travel before you leave. Don't let a dog ride with its head out the window; wind, sand, dirt, and gravel might damage its eyes permanently. Just crack the glass enough for his nose. See that the pet exercises regularly. Highway comfort stations and rest stops are excellent places to halt for a spell and unwind, and many have the bonus of being scenic. Don't forget your pet's water and food dish. And never, never leave a dog or cat in the car on a hot day, even with the window cracked open. The blazing Texas sun can heat the inside of a car to more than 115 F. (46 C.) in a matter of minutes.

HOTELS AND MOTELS. *General tips.* Always make advance reservations whenever possible. Otherwise, you are sure to waste time and energy at least once in your trip looking for accommodations that, in the end, may not suit your needs. If you don't have reservations for the night, start looking for a hotel or motel early, say four o'clock. Remember that special sporting or cultural events of which you are unaware may cause all the vacant rooms in a city to disappear on a certain day—the day you might arrive in town without a reservation.

When you make advance reservations, advise the hotel or motel operator when you expect to arrive. Most hostels will not keep reservations after 6:00 P.M., so if you want to be absolutely sure to have a room when you arrive late, give the number of one of your credit cards over the phone to pay for the lodging in advance. Many chain or associated motels and hotels will make reservations with their affiliates at your next destination.

Whether to choose a hotel or a motel for your lodging is a difficult decision, since the amenities in each category are so similar. But in general, you will find that hotels offer a bit more personalized service to their guests. Also (in general) hotels run a bit more expensive than motels of comparable quality. Many hotels have one-day laundry and dry-cleaning service, whereas motels are more prone to offer a coin-operated laundromat, if anything. Room service is rare in motels but almost always available in hotels. Seldom, if ever, do you have to pay for parking at a motel; in hotels, there is usually a charge for use of the hotel garage, in addition to the tip you give the parking attendant. You won't find porters and bellmen in motels (unless you are in a resort area), but, on the other hand, you will probably be able to park quite near your room. Television, bedside telephones, and in-room toilets, baths, and showers are standard fare for motels and hotels in all price categories. Many have swimming pools, even in downtown areas. As for motels and motor inns in the urban areas, you will find that they offer about the same conveniences as the older, sometimes more elegant hotels, the only exception being more personalized service in hotels.

Hotel and motel chains. In addition to the hundreds of fine independent motels and hotels in Texas, many lodging establishments belong to national or regional chains. Two advantages to staying in chain motels are the ease of making future reservations and the great degree of standardization among the affiliates. You know almost exactly what kind of room you will have tomorrow night by looking at the one you have tonight. The main hotel chains in Texas are *Hilton Inns, Hyatt, Marriott,* and *Sheraton.* The major motel chains are *Best Western, Holiday Inn, Howard Johnson's, La Quinta, Quality Inns, Ramada Inns, Days Inns,* and *TraveLodge.* In all the hotel and motel chains mentioned above, you can expect at the least to find rooms with full baths, color TV sets, telephones, desks, carpeting, and usually double or queen-sized beds. Budget motel chains also exist in Texas, and they offer almost the same amenities (right down to the swimming pool) but at a substantial savings. Economical chains include *Rodeway Inns, Comfort Inns,* and *Motel 6.*

Categories. Hotels and motels in all the Fodor's guidebooks to the U.S.A. are divided into categories, arranged primarily by price but also taking into consideration the degree of comfort, the amount of service, and the atmosphere that will surround you in the establishment of your choice. The dollar ranges for each category are clearly stated before the listing of establishments for each city. Remember that prices and ratings are subject to change on rather short notice. We should also point out that many fine hotels and motels had to be omitted for lack of space.

Super Deluxe. A category reserved for only a few hotels that render deluxe accommodation in a special atmosphere of glamour, good taste, and dignity. The hotel will probably be a meeting place for local high society. The tops in everything, including price.

Deluxe. The minimum facilities must include bath and shower in all rooms, suites available, a well-appointed restaurant and bar, room service, color TV and telephone in room, air conditioning and heat, and ample personalized service including laundry service if it is a hotel. In a deluxe motel or motor inn, fewer services may be available by employees and more by automatic machines.

Expensive. All rooms must have bath or shower, TV and telephone, attractive furnishings, and heat and air conditioning, and there must be a restaurant within or next door to the establishment. Motels in this category may have laundromats, which should be in a convenient location.

Moderate. Each room will have a bath or shower and (unless in a resort area) TV and a telephone; a restaurant or coffee shop should be nearby. Functional lodging, perhaps not in the best location.

Inexpensive. Almost always the rooms will have a bath or a shower, but occasionally such facilities might be down the hall. TV and telephone may be included, optional, or unavailable. Clean, functional rooms are the minimum. In *Motel 6* and *Rodeway* there is always a pool. Motels in this price range are usually good bargains; in hotels you might want to look over the room before you take it.

 DINING OUT. Except for a few fancy establishments in Houston, evening meals are the only ones for which you should occasionally worry about reservations. To make matters complicated, more and more restaurants refuse to accept reservations, preferring instead to have you sit in their bar or lounge drinking expensive liquor until a table is ready. On a busy night (Friday, Saturday, Sunday) you should call up before leaving your hotel and ask how long a wait there will be before getting a table. Seven o'clock is usually when the largest crowd arrives.

Texas is a state for casual dress. Few are the restaurants where a man would be turned away for want of a tie. "No shoes, no shirt, no service" is a much more common warning to customers than "Gentlemen need jackets." Women should encounter even fewer problems as long as they don't wear shorts or jeans to a swanky restaurant in Houston. If you are traveling with children, you may want to call ahead to a restaurant to see whether it offers a children's menu. Lower-priced plates for kids are rapidly disappearing.

Restaurant Categories. Restaurants in Houston and Galveston are classified in this volume according to type of cuisine served and the price for a typical meal (without extras). Limitations of space make it impossible to list every establishment. Instead, you will find what we consider to be the best selections in each category. As a rule, prices in metropolitan areas are higher than those in rural regions. Although the various restaurant categories are the same throughout the Fodor's series of guides, the prices in each category may differ from region to region. You will see the dollar ranges for each category clearly stated before the listings of the restaurants. Menus are volatile; prices might go up after press time. In all our categories, the price range *does not* include cocktails, wines, cover charges, tips, or extravagant house specialties.

Deluxe. This category denotes an outstanding restaurant with a lavish or particularly attractive atmosphere. These restaurants are indeed difficult to get out of for less than $15–$20 per person, even if you skip dessert and alcohol and order the cheapest thing on the menu. Deluxe restaurants should have a superb wine list and a good bar, excellent service, and delectable food.

Expensive. In addition to the expected dishes, an expensive restaurant will offer one or two house specialties, a good wine list, cocktails, air conditioning, good service, and a good atmosphere for dining in comfort.

Moderate. Cocktails or beer available, air-conditioned, better-than-average service, and a reputation for wholesome food.

Inexpensive. Good food at bargain prices. Frequently there are house specialties, too. Availability of beer, wine, and drinks may vary. Air conditioning, tables (or tables and counter), good service. Cafeterias are good bets.

 TIPPING. Giving tips expresses your appreciation for service well received. You should reward courteous, efficient service fairly. Likewise, when you receive poor or surly service, you should express polite dissatisfaction by reducing or withholding your tip. In many service establishments, especially restaurants, waiters and waitresses are paid far below the prevailing minimum wage. Much of their income depends on the tips they receive. This system is intended to induce good servce. But we, as customers, must remember that courteous and efficient service is all that should be required for an employee to receive the standard gratuity. A waiter can render extra-special attention to your desires only if that attention is not at the expense of other customers. When you get such special attention, it merits extra compensation.

The standard tip for restaurant, bar, and cocktail-lounge service is 15% on the amount of the bill *before* taxes. Do not include the tax when figuring your tip. Good service, however, might be more easily rewarded by simply dividing the pretax amount by six and then rounding off to the nearest quarter. This calculation provides a tip of about 16.7% and is often quicker to determine than figuring exactly 15% when you're in a hurry or if you're not an arithmetic whiz. Similarly, if service was not quite up to par, dividing the pretax amount of the

FACTS AT YOUR FINGERTIPS 11

bill by 8 or 9 will render 12.5% or 11.1%. You can be assured that the difference will be noted by the employee. In many Texas establishments, a service charge (usually 15%) is included in the bill for parties of six or more. When it is, an extra 5% tip is necessary only if you made many special requests or if you genuinely appreciated the waiter's attention. When you drink something at a bar or at the counter in a restaurant, leave at least 10% (25¢ minimum). There is no tipping in fast-food restaurants, self-service eateries, and outdoor concession stands.

A hotel bellman gets $1 per suitcase, unless you load him down with a lot of extras. If you do, give that extra $1 or $2. Doormen and parking attendants usually receive $1 for parking or fetching a car. For short stays in hotels and motels it is not necessary to tip the maid unless you throw a party in your room or make a mess. If you stay longer than two nights, leave the maid about $1 a day, on the last day of your stay. Room service gets about 15% of the bill before tax (but be sure to check the bill first for any included service charge). Tip barbers and hairdressers 15%, minimum $2. The person who washes your hair gets $1 (unless it's the barber or hairdresser who does it). Manicurists get 10% of their bill, and so should shoeshiners.

Tip 15% on taxi fares. If the driver helps you with your luggage, give 25¢ per item for loading and unloading and 50¢ per item if he helps you carry them any distance. On the train, give 15% to dining-car waiters and $1 a night to the sleeping-car attendant. Remember, there is never any tipping on a plane. Tip airport porters and redcaps the same as hotel bellmen for carrying your luggage.

SENIOR-CITIZEN AND STUDENT DISCOUNTS. Since there is no uniformity in age-related discounts, the only thing to do is to ask each time you purchase an admission. Some attractions in Texas—especially museums, cultural spectacles, and movie houses—offer discounted admissions to senior citizens (generally 65 and older) and to bona-fide students. Some proof of age and affiliation will be required. Usually, places offering student discounts will be more strict—they may require a high school or college ID or possibly an international student travel card. Most cinemas now require the student to provide proof of age and then to purchase a special student pass in order to get student admission at that theater. Few, if any, discounts remain for air, rail, or bus tickets. One place to look for special senior-citizen rates and privileges, though, is the state and national parks.

DRINKING LAWS. The minimum age in Texas for consumption and possession of alcoholic beverages is 21. Other liquor laws vary from county to county. Out of 254 Texas counties, 69 are wholly dry—that is, no alcoholic beverages are sold. In 14 counties, only beer or beer and wine are marketed. In 171 counties, which include all the major cities, the status is wet, at least in part.

Bottled distilled liquor must be purchased in state-licensed package stores, which may be open from 10:00 A.M. to 9:00 P.M. except on Sundays and certain holidays. Beer and wine can be bought in liquor stores, supermarkets, and convenience stores between 7:00 A.M. and midnight, except on Sundays, when beer and wine sales begin at noon.

BUSINESS HOURS, HOLIDAYS, AND LOCAL TIME. Houston and Galveston, like most of the rest of Texas, are on Central Standard Time from the last Sunday in October to the last Sunday in April. (CST is the same as Chicago: one hour earlier than New York and the East Coast, six hours earlier than GMT.) El Paso is on Mountain Standard Time, one hour earlier. As in the rest of the United States, on the last Sunday in April the clocks are advanced one hour to establish Daylight Savings Time. On the last Sunday in October, they are turned back an hour.

Texas banking hours are generally from 9:00 A.M. to 2:00 P.M., but you can usually find "mini-lobbies" and drive-in windows in major banks that are open before and after the main-lobby schedule. Most large banks operate their drive-in facilities on Saturday, too. Remote self-service stations are now being used by banks; these require bank or credit cards and are accessible 24 hours a day seven days a week in most shopping centers and some grocery stores. Currency-exchange services are found only in the larger banks in the main cities, so be sure to change foreign monies in sufficient amounts or carry your funds in U.S.-dollar traveler's checks.

Shops and boutiques usually open at 8:30 or 9:00 A.M.; department stores and shopping malls, at 10:00. Many malls, and some stores, stay open until 9:00 P.M. Otherwise, the closing hour is generally 5:30. Some now maintain limited hours on Sunday. Most professional offices, businesses, and government bureaus open at 8:00 A.M. and close at 5:00 P.M.

The banks, most businesses, and some restaurants are closed on the following holidays: New Year's Day; Presidents Day, mid-February; Easter; Memorial Day, end of May; Independence Day, July 4; Labor Day, early September; Thanksgiving Day, late November; and Christmas, December 25. The banks and some other establishments are also closed on Columbus Day in mid-October and Veterans Day in early November. Texas state holidays are also celebrated, but they usually affect only state-government offices. Texas Independence Day, a big hoo-ha, is March 2nd.

POSTAGE. Don't forget that U.S. domestic airmail rates apply to Canada and Mexico, too. The current airmail rate is 22¢ for letters of 1 oz. (28 g.) or less and 14¢ for postcards. International airmail postcard rate is 33¢. Airmail rates for the Caribbean, Central America, and parts of South America are less than regular international rates: 39¢. International aerogrammes cost 36¢—but do not enclose anything in them.

SPORTS. Participant Sports. Along the gulf coast you will find **sailing, boating, yachting, waterskiing, windsurfing,** and outstanding **fishing.** Galveston offers all, but you also should investigate northeast to the Bolivar Peninsula, known for its openness and isolation, and southwest over San Luis Pass to Freeport. Clear Lake, south of Houston, empties into upper Galveston Bay; together they form one of the best water recreation zones in America.

If you enjoy knocking little white balls around beautiful countryside, don't leave your **golf** clubs behind when you visit the Houston–Galveston area. Championship courses abound, including many carved amid the piney woods of this east Texas region.

Texans are into **tennis** in a big way. Several professional players have come from Texas, and many are resident pros in the Houston/Galveston region. Excellent resort courts and private tennis clubs are available, but for casual exercise you'll find free courts in almost any public park.

Hunting is excellent along the sea-rim marshes of the upper Texas coast during the November-January deer season. Quail season is October–January, and three major flyways bring migratory waterfowl in abundance, making the area a mecca for birders and hunters alike. For regulations, request the free *Guide to Texas Hunting and Sport Fishing Regulations* from the Texas Parks and Wildlife Department, 4200 Smith School Road, Austin, TX 78744; 800–792 –1112 (in Texas).

There are more than 250 species of saltwater fish waiting for your bait or lure along the gulf coast. You can angle from boats, by wading the flats, or from piers and jetties. Two major freshwater lakes lie within a 30-minute drive north of downtown Houston.

Runners should definitely bring their togs and shoes. Houston has several hike and bike trails along bayous and through parks, and Galveston's seawall is a happy running and jogging ground. **Bicycling** is also gaining ground every year in Texas, especially in the cities. Of course, **horseback riding** is popular in the most cowboy of all states. Western-style riding prevails. English riding, show riding, and steeplechase now can be found at a new facility in west Houston, for both observers and participants.

Spectator Sports. One word that just about sums up this category is **football.** From August to the end of January, the football fever runs amok in the state. During your trip you can measure just how passionate and serious a disease this is by counting the bumper stickers praising the Dallas Cowboys, the Houston Oilers, or any of the hundreds of university and high school teams. College football season runs concurrent with the professional schedule. Most of the Southwest Conference football teams are based in Texas. For some real Texan excitement around a real American experience, take in a game in one of the enormous stadiums bedecked with Astroturf and bright lights. It is unforgettable.

Baseball follows football today as the most popular spectator sport, but it is still the most all-American one. Professional games are held in Dallas and Houston. Good college encounters can be found during the spring.

Rodeos are held regularly in both large and small communities all over the state. Check local newspapers and magazines for times and locations. If you are visiting Houston, you can take in a rodeo in nearby Simonton every Saturday night, kicked off by a typical Texas barbeque.

CAMPING AND RV FACILITIES. Camping facilities are widespread in Texas, and more are springing up each year. National parks, state parks, municipal parks, as well as private firms and individuals, provide campgrounds for tents and hookups for recreational vehicles.

Of 90 state parks and monuments across Texas, 49 have at a minimum electricity and water hookups, restrooms, and cooking facilities, and some of those also have sewage hookups and showers, swimming pools, and tennis courts. Hookups cost an additional fee of about $5 to $7 a day. Reservations for camping spots in state parks are strongly recommended, especially during the summer.

There are no municipal campgrounds within the Houston city limits and only one in Harris County. Galveston has camping in one state park, on the west side of the island, one county park, on the Bolivar peninsula, and one RV Park, at the end of Seawall Boulevard at 7–Mile Road (information: 409–766–2411). Camping is not allowed on the open beaches.

Private campgrounds and RV parks are often small and here-now-gone-tomorrow enterprises. That is not to say that they offer fewer or poorer services, just that they are more difficult to locate. Look for private campgrounds near the state parks and recreation areas, since their private counterparts will be trying to capitalize on the excess of visitors to the parks. One chain campground that is an exception to this is *Kampgrounds of America* (KOA), a series of well-maintained RV and camping parks near recreation areas and cities. For more information, write KOA, Inc., P.O. Box 30558, Billings, MT 59114, or check the local phone book for a nearby listing. KOA grounds often have grocery stores, telephones, and swimming pools.

For more camping information, you may want to contact a Texas tourist bureau (see *Tourist Information,* above) to get a copy of the *Texas Public Campgrounds Guide.*

THEME PARKS. *Astroworld* and *Waterworld,* at the southern edge of metro Houston via South Main Street, draw crowds throughout the summer and on spring and fall weekends. Stage shows mix with more than 80 rides at Astroworld. Waterworld's 15 acres have waterfalls, wave pools, chutes, rapids, etc.—a nice place to be when Houston swelters mid-year.

A new $40 million theme park, *Fame City,* opened in mid-1986 in far southwest Houston. Included are a 10-acre outdoor facility called Water Works and a 25-acre air-conditioned building filled with sports, games, rides, eateries, and more. While not billed as a theme park, the *Alabama–Coushatta Indian Reserva-*

tion offers good family entertainment north of Houston between Livingston and Woodville via U.S. highways 59 north and 190 east.

For other theme parks throughout the state, see *Fodor's Texas* guidebook.

 HINTS TO HANDICAPPED TRAVELERS. All federal and state and most city office buildings; the state universities, colleges, and parks; and most municipal street departments have instituted, or are in the process of instituting, special privileges and facilities for the handicapped. More and more curbs, especially in downtown areas, have antislip ramps for wheelchairs. Reserved parking spaces are often seen. And public bathrooms and toilets have special stalls. Most businesses have been following suit.

Many hotel and motel chains, including *Holiday Inn, Hyatt, Ramada,* and *Sheraton,* have made efforts to provide special rooms for the handicapped in most of their establishments. Be sure to ask the hotel or motel if they have special accommodations when you call to make reservations.

Many state parks have paved, level nature trails that easily accommodate handicapped visitors. Call the individual park before your visit, to find out for sure. For travel tips for the handicapped, write the following organizations: Consumer Information Center, Pueblo, CO 81109; Society for the Advancement of Travel for the Handicapped, 26 Court St., Brooklyn, NY 11242.

Access to the National Parks is a handbook that describes facilities for the handicapped at all national parks. It costs $3.50 and is obtainable from the U.S. Government Printing Office, Washington, D.C. 20402. For a free copy of *Access Amtrak,* a train guide for the handicapped, write Amtrak, National Railroad and Passenger Corporation, 400 N. Capitol St., N.W., Washington, D.C. 20001.

HOUSTON

CAROL BISBEE BARRINGTON

Carol Bisbee Barrington, an award-winning travel writer and photographer, lives in Houston and specializes in magazine and newspaper feature articles on Texas. She is the author of a book, Day Trips from Houston, *and is a member of the Society of American Travel Writers. John Ashby Wilburn, who produced part of the Practical Information section, is the Editor of* VIVA, *and has been the Managing Editor for* Houston City *magazine.*

Given Houston's national media billing some years ago as "The Golden Buckle on the Sun Belt," visitors often come to this young city with high expectations and strong misconceptions. In short, the city they experience is not usually the utopia they expect.

17

First of all, is this Texas? The mind's eye often equates the Lone Star State with sagebrush, and many visitors are amazed by the vast acres of forest, water, and green pastureland surrounding Houston. The second blow is the weather—subtropical, changeable, and often uncomfortable. From its founding as a real-estate development in 1836 until the mid-1950s, Houston was actually considered an unhealthy place to live. It is no coincidence that the city's first spurt of significant growth came with the advent of affordable commercial and residential air-conditioning.

Clean and almost starkly modern with scant respect for restrictions, also-rans, and yesterday, Houston may well be the last hangout in continental America for the rugged individualist, a lodestone to the entrepreneur eager to seek his fortune amid the canyons of commerce. Unhampered by zoning, planning, or strong unions, Houston from 1970 to 1983 grew seven days a week wherever the developers' dollars have beckoned, covering thousands of acres with cement and buildings that weren't there the month before. Visitors should expect some tarnish on that golden belt buckle, however. The city's fortunes began falling along with international oil prices in 1983, and the ensuing ripples of recession have brought on a rash of bankruptcy and foreclosure proceedings that continue at this writing.

As modern as Houston looks, it doesn't always work. Those same elements which nurtured its enormous growth have created "jumble city." Islands of magnificent architecture often look out on slums or are built to the very edge of sidewalks, forever forcing traffic through four-lane funnels. Many ordinary municipal services such as adequate police protection, cheap and reliable public transportation, and decent roads are in very short supply. Human planning in terms of new parks, green belts, historic preservation, and the like has been very far down the list of civic priorities.

You'll need two basics: a car to get around and plenty of money or "plastic" to enjoy the city's swinging lifestyle. Houston's heyday as one of the least expensive entertainment cities in America is long gone, victim of inflation and the proliferation of corporate expense accounts.

And it helps to understand the natives. Less conservative than Dallasites and far less relaxed than San Antonians, Houstonians seem to live in their cars, always en route somewhere. And they come in several major guises, ranging from the corporate businessperson (often a transplant from California or New York) to the redneck. The latter is a Texian term for local boy whose daddy probably farmed some and raised cattle on the land that today sprouts subdivisions and shopping centers. He is easily identifiable by his cowboy boots and well-washed jeans, a name like Bubba or Jim Bob tooled into the back of his belt, and the guns on the rack in his pickup.

Enjoy both types. The first keeps contemporary Houston prosperous, and the second gives it character.

And "folks talk funny here," as a visiting friend once commented. Yankee or Michigan dialects aside, the local patois is a unique blend of black, Chicano, and lazy-South accents and can be difficult to understand. Just ask folks to slow down until you get your ears in tune.

On the Banks of Buffalo Bayou

"The town of Houston is located at a point on the river which must ever command the trade of the largest and richest portion of Texas." So did those first promos put out in the eastern press by the Allen Brothers sell the sizzle of their new real-estate speculation in August, 1836. That river the ad refers to was muddy, narrow, and barely navigable Buffalo Bayou, and the town was nonexistent—just half a league (four thousand acres) of coastal prairie the Allen Brothers bought for a thousand dollars down and four thousand dollars more whenever.

Their timing was as good as their promotion. Sam Houston's forces had just defeated Santa Anna and his vastly superior Mexican army near this dubious hunk of real estate, and suddenly the fledgling Republic of Texas was ripe for settlement and commercial exploitation. Naming the new town-to-be after the hero of the revolution was a genius of a higher sort, and when the seat of government moved to Houston from West Columbia in 1837, the settlement began to earn its promotional label: "The City of the Future."

Things haven't changed much in the nearly century and a half since. Houston today is a real-estate developer's dream of opportunity, in spite of the current recession. Those short, square downtown blocks laid out by the Allen Brothers now sport massive skyscrapers, one of the most contemporary civic panoramas in America. Downtown Houston has become an architectural showcase.

Still bounded on the north by the natural bend of Buffalo Bayou but otherwise encircled by freeways, the downtown district is slowly becoming a "people place" in spite of itself. New parks and plazas, plus fun things like plays, programs, art shows, etc., are beginning to curb the 4:30 P.M. exodus to the suburbs, and weekend festivals often lure folks back into town. Do be aware, however, that few people actually *live* downtown and that after dark this core of the city is usually a ghost town, a dangerous place to wander. Nor is it possible to see it all by foot at one time. Best make a windshield tour first and then either explore on foot or take one of the walking tours conducted by the Greater Houston Preservation Alliance on the third Wednesday (12 noon) of each month, starting from Milam and Preston; $1 fee.

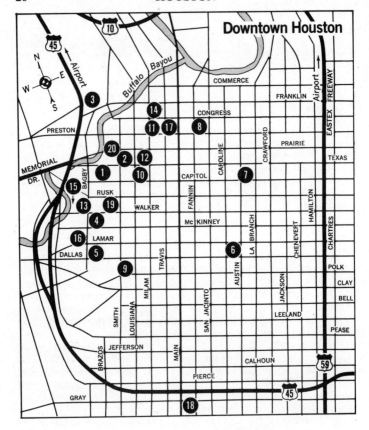

Downtown Houston

Points of Interest

1) Albert Thomas Convention and Exhibit Center
2) Alley Theater
3) Amtrak Station
4) City Hall
5) Doubletree Hotel
6) Four Seasons Hotel
7) Greyhound Terminal
8) Harris County Courthouse Square
9) Hyatt-Regency Hotel
10) Jesse H. Jones Hall for the Performing Arts
11) Kennedy Bakery (La Carafe)
12) Lancaster Hotel
13) Music Hall
14) Old Cotton Exchange
15) Sam Houston Coliseum
16) Sam Houston Park
17) Sweeny-Coombs-Fredericks Building
18) Trailways Bus Terminal
19) Tranquility Park
20) Wortham Theater Center

Plans to develop Buffalo Bayou into a residential-recreation corridor park have not yet moved forward. For now, both the bayou and Allen's Landing are unremarkable and, aside from their history, have little to offer of tourist interest. The area bounded by Commerce, Fannin, Texas, and Louisiana Streets was the heart of old Houston, but only a handful of the original buildings remain. Best of the lot are the Old Cotton Exchange (1884), 202 Travis; the old Kennedy Bakery (1860s), now La Carafe, 813 Congress, thought to be the oldest commercial building still on its original site; the Pillot Building (1860), 1016 Congress, the last of many iron-fronted buildings in the city; and the Sweeny-Coombs-Fredericks Building (1889), 301 Main, a marvelous Victorian recently restored by Harris County.

If you're in this district at lunchtime, stop for some Cajun cuisine at the Cloisters, an inexpensive cafeteria-style lunchroom operated by the Altar Guild of Christ Church at the northeast corner of Fannin and Texas. Built in 1893, this is the oldest church in the city and the second oldest in the state. Just ask at the church office for a tour and a glimpse of its famed Tiffany window. Incidentally, that Cajun food comes from Treebeard's, four blocks away on Travis in Old Market Square.

For a look at today's Houston, park your car in the Civic Center garage (directional signs on Smith, Bagby, Rusk, and Walker) and begin at Tranquillity Park. A Bicentennial project commemorating the Apollo space flights, this futuristic oasis is an ideal vantage point from which to survey the monoliths of downtown. Among those within walking distance west of Main Street are Pennzoil Place (1976), twin towers separated by a twelve-foot space and still one of the most distinctive buildings in town; the Texas Commerce Tower (1982), at seventy-five stories the world's tallest composite tube tower, with Miró's *Personage and Birds* for comic relief in its front plaza; One Shell Plaza (1971), at one time the tallest reinforced-concrete building west of the Mississippi; and Allied Bank Plaza (1983), fifty stories of reflective glass a wag once described as a Dunhill lighter. From the air this last building curves like a fat dollar sign, appropriate since its estimated value is approximately $160 million.

Many of these buildings overlook tiny Sam Houston Park, where the Harris County Heritage Society gives guided tours of five historic buildings (see the *Tours* section below).

Tranquillity Park is the threshold of Civic Center, home to the Albert Thomas Convention and Visitor's Center, Wortham Theater Center, the Alley Theatre, and the Jesse H. Jones Hall for the Performing Arts. The underground garage serves these and other facilities. Walk around the blocks bounded by Louisiana and Texas streets—you may catch the Houston Symphony in a noontime concert in Oscar Holcombe Plaza in front of the Alley.

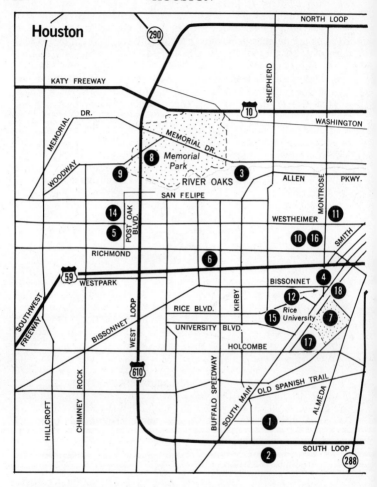

Points of Interest

1) Astrodome
2) Astroworld
3) Bayou Bend Branch, Museum of Fine Arts
4) Contemporary Arts Museum
5) Galleria
6) Greenway Plaza
7) Hermann Park, including the Museum of Medical Science, Museum of Natural Science, Hermann Park Zoo, and Hermann Park Garden Center

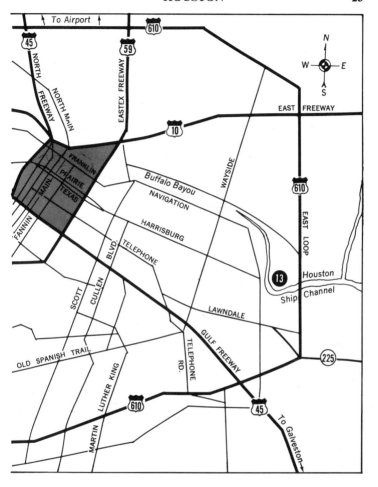

8) Houston Arboretum and Nature Center
9) Inn on the Park Hotel
10) Menil Collection (Museum)
11) Montrose Neighborhood
12) Museum of Fine Arts
13) Port of Houston

14) Post Oak Shopping Sector
15) Rice University Institute for the Arts
16) Rothko Chapel
17) Texas Medical Center
18) Warwick Hotel

The new Wortham Theater Center is magnificent and well worth touring; call 237–1439 for information. Jones Hall, however, is open only during performances, but it is worth the price of a ticket to see this building's interior. A fascinating sculpture, *Gemini II,* by Richard Lippold, soars through the upper reaches of the lobby. Made of several thousand hexagonal rods from three to six feet long, each polished to a jewel finish, it is suspended from the lobby ceiling by stainless-steel wire. The sculpture echoes the curves and angles of the building, and none of the rods touches another.

A vast warren of underground tunnels connects most of the major downtown office buildings, but not always in a direct route. "You are here" directories help you find your way through the maze of intersections and retail businesses. The only sidewalk public access to the tunnels at present is at the Allied Bank Plaza, 1000 Louisiana. Nice to know: Most of the street-level lobbies of these new buildings are "walk-through," and you can enter the tunnel system via their down escalators.

West of Main is another world, best described as the Phoenix of Houston. Less than four years ago downtown "stopped" at San Jacinto, and a wasteland of warehouses and shlock began. Now the new First City Tower, with its diagonal line and plazas, rises here, followed by the first beauties of the thirty-three block Houston Center development, the new Gulf Tower, and the Four Seasons Hotel. Across the street is the Park in Houston Center, the first major retail project built in downtown since the mid-1950s. One walk here, and the Allen Brothers' prophetic billing of Houston as the city of the future comes true for the tourist.

The new $200-million George R. Brown Houston Convention Center is under construction at the eastern end of Houston Center, immediately adjacent to the Eastex Freeway (U.S. 59 North). On the other side of the freeway is Houston's rapidly expanding Chinatown, a multiblock complex bounded by McKinney, Rusk, St. Emanuel, and Chartres streets.

Down to the Gulf in Ships

Even though Houston lies fifty miles inland from the Gulf of Mexico, it is the nation's third-largest port, owing to a forty-foot-deep ship channel dug through shallow Galveston Bay and up Buffalo Bayou in 1915. You can watch the action in the busy turning basin from the free observation deck on the top of Wharf 9. Just go through Gate 8 from Clinton Drive, east of downtown and accessible from the 610 loop. A boat tour of the port must be reserved in advance (see the *Tours* section below). Crews from the ships as well as Houstonians love two watering holes nearby: Shanghai Red's, 8501 Cypress, for its free happy-hour and seafood buffet every weeknight except Thursday, when a Mexican buffet featuring fajitas is the draw; and the Athens Bar and Grill, 8037 Clinton, for its Greek music and dancing.

Next stop east of town is the San Jacinto Battleground State Historic Park (see the *Historic Sites* section below), where you can tour a battleship, visit a museum, and catch a 360-degree view of the surrounding countryside. After that, follow the road east to the free Lunchburg Ferry for a short ride back and forth across one neck of the bay. En route back to Houston, swing by Gilley's, 4500 Spencer Highway. Long before it was the setting for the movie *Urban Cowboy,* Gilley's was one of the top country-and-western hangouts in this part of Texas and the action level remains high.

South of Downtown

The Texas Medical Center, three miles due south of downtown via Fannin and Main streets, is a city unto itself. More than twenty major health facilities are crowded onto 180 acres, among them the M. D. Anderson Hospital and Tumor Institute, famed for its cancer treatments, and the Texas Heart Institute (see the *Tours* section below). Just getting to the Med Center from downtown is one of the quiet pleasures of the city. From the Mecom Fountain at the Warwick Hotel to University Boulevard, South Main is lined with marvelous old oaks as it goes past Hermann Park.

South Main and the 610 Loop South are the main arteries to Astrodomain—Astroworld, Astrohall, and the Astrodome. Tours of the latter are interesting, but it's much better to see the place in action. Check with the box office, 799–9500, to see who's playing what. When it opened in 1965, the Astrodome was called the eighth wonder of the world, for as the first domed stadium larger than a football field, it was the prototype of things to come.

Houston's southern section extends twenty-five miles south from downtown via the Gulf Freeway (I–45) to the Nassau Bay/Clear Lake area and includes the Johnson Space Center. Weekends are nice here—there's usually a speedboat or sailboat race on Clear Lake, and the return trip can include a venture into the wilderness of Armand Bayou (see the *Parks* section).

Houston's Other Business Centers

Like satellite cities, Greenway Plaza and the Galleria sprout among the trees west of downtown. Begun in 1967, the 127-acre Greenway Plaza encompasses ten office towers, apartments, a Stouffer's hotel, and

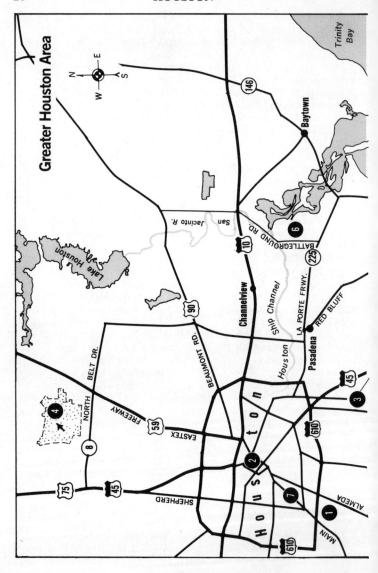

Greater Houston Area

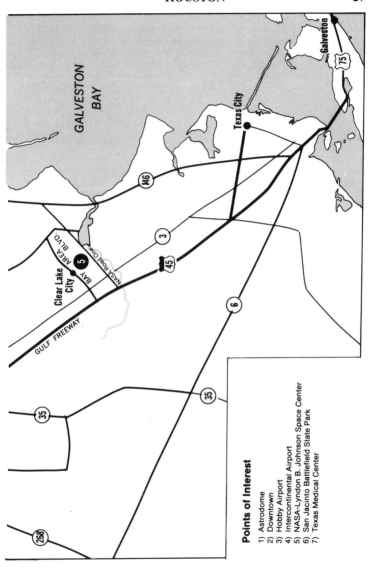

Points of Interest

1) Astrodome
2) Downtown
3) Hobby Airport
4) Intercontinental Airport
5) NASA-Lyndon B. Johnson Space Center
6) San Jacinto Battlefield State Park
7) Texas Medical Center

an excellent multi-sport and entertainment facility, the Summit. You
can't miss the place—just look for high-rises and a cluster of big
American flags near the Buffalo Speedway exit from the Southwest
Freeway (U.S. 59 South).

The Galleria is both a specific place and an area, the latter also called
the Magic Circle. These few golden blocks just west of the 610 Loop
in the Westheimer–San Felipe–South Post Oak locale sport the finest
shopping in the city as well as high-rise headquarters for numerous
international businesses. Amazing that little more than twenty years
ago, the corner of South Post Oak and Westheimer was an open field
edged by a little-used blacktop road.

What a difference some millions can make! First came Sakowitz and
then Joske's. Neiman's followed, and by 1965 the design of the adjoin-
ing and lavish Galleria had begun. The doors opened in 1971 on the
most elegant shopping mall in southwestern America, containing a
luxury hotel and three tiers of shops surrounding an indoor ice rink.
An expansion five years later brought Galleria II, with a second hotel,
Lord & Taylor and Marshall Field, and this part of Houston became
a destination in itself. Galleria III opened in 1986, adding Macy's and
numerous small but glitzy boutiques to the complex. Most of the stores
employ multilingual personnel, so strong is the international traffic
here.

Suburbia

Some other areas of Houston crop up in conversations often enough
to warrant some information here. The River Oaks section northeast
of the Galleria and just south of Memorial Park is world-famous for
lavish and beautiful homes. The Memorial area follows Memorial
Drive west from Memorial Park on its curving ramble west to Texas
6, passing numerous small enclaves of elegant homes. The Town and
Country Shopping Center is near the western end of the Memorial
district and borders what will someday be a vast Outer Belt Highway,
twelve miles from the central business district. At present, most of the
Outer Belt exists only on highway-department dream maps, the excep-
tions being the Beltway 8 bridge over the Houston Ship Channel and
an approximately eight-mile stretch between U.S. 59 and I–45 near the
airport. This latter road forms the North Belt business district and, as
it merges with I–45, passes Greenspoint Mall.

Even farther north, FM 1960 arcs across the northern reaches of
Harris County from Humble through the Champions area en route to
the Fort Bend County line in the southwest. Although portions of the
1960 area will probably be annexed by Houston in the near future, for

now it remains one of the fastest-growing commercial and residential areas in America but with little of special interest to the visitor.

PRACTICAL INFORMATION
FOR HOUSTON

HOW TO GET THERE. By car. As I–10 crosses Texas from the Louisiana border on the east to the New Mexico border on the west, it passes through the heart of Houston. U.S. 59 runs northeast to southwest, and I–45 northwest to southeast.

The approximate driving times to Houston from other cities, in hours, are: New Orleans 7; Dallas 5; Galveston 1; Corpus Christi 4; South Padre Island 7½; Austin 3½; and San Antonio 4.

By train. *Amtrak* passenger service connects Houston three times a week with New Orleans, Los Angeles, and San Antonio. The station is at 902 Washington Ave., at the intersection of Bagby; 224–1577. Reservations also can be made at (800) 872–7245.

By air. Confirm in advance which of the city's two airports you will be using. Some airlines have flights into both.

W. P. Hobby Airport is 9 mi. southeast of downtown via I–45 and Broadway Blvd.; 643–4597. A new garage adjacent to the terminal has relieved serious parking congestion.

Houston Intercontinental Airport is 15 mi. north of downtown, accessible from either I–45 or U.S. 59 via North Belt.

Between the two airports, Houston is served by some 25 airlines. Domestic service is provided by *American Continental, Delta, Northwest, Piedmont, Southwest, Pan American, TranStar, TransWorld, United,* and *US Air.* International service is provided by several of the above, as well as *Aeromexico, Air France, Aviateca, British Caledonian, Cayman, KLM, Lufthansa, TACA, TAN SAHSA,* and *Viasa.* Several commuter airlines also fly into both airports.

By bus. Houston is served by *Greyhound Bus Lines,* 2121 Main (759–6500).

TELEPHONES. The area code for Houston and most of the surrounding area is 713. You do not need to dial the area code if it is the same as the one from which you are dialing. However, some of the 713 area numbers outside Houston require that you dial a "1" first, then the seven digit calling number. A new area code, 409, now covers some outlying areas, such as Beaumont, Galveston, Sealy, and the Liberty-Dayton sectors. If your call requires a "1" or the new area code, an apologetic voice will tell you so in electronic pear-shaped tones after you have dialed. For local information within the 713 calling area, dial 1411. For directory information outside the 713 area, dial the area code, then 555-1212. If you need operator assistance, dial "0" (zero). Pay-telephone calls are 25¢.

HOTELS AND MOTELS. Few cities can match Houston when it comes to accommodations. The economic vitality of the past decade has brought a hotel-motel boom of surprising proportions, and yet room costs are generally somewhat below what you would find in many other major American cities. The challenge is finding the right place to stay in terms of location and budget. Fortunately, there are fine choices all over town, particularly in the *Super Deluxe* and *Deluxe* categories.

Some hotels, such as those in the Galleria, are destinations in themselves. Others are convenient to downtown, the Texas Medical Center, or a specific business district. We've noted general areas along with addresses so you can select a hotel near where you will be spending most of your time. We've also noted those which offer complimentary transportation to the in-town airline terminals, Medical Center, or shopping, and there is a special category for accommodations worth checking for long-term stays in the Medical Center. With careful selections you may be able to get along without a rental car after all.

Also, Houston is a businessman's city, and even the swankiest hotels have low occupancy rates on weekends. Most of the rates noted are slashed from 30 to 60% on special one- or two-night weekend packages, with some nice extras like champagne or breakfast tossed in for good measure. If you'll be in town over a Friday or Saturday night, ask about these special packages when you reserve. Many hotels and motels also offer family plans, free cribs, and free accommodations for children sharing the parents' room.

Hotel rates are based on double occupancy, European Plan (no meals). Categories, determined by price, are: *Super Deluxe,* $150 and up; *Deluxe,* $100 to $150; *Expensive,* $75 to $120; *Moderate,* $55–85; *Inexpensive,* $55 and under.

Most of America's major hotel and motel chains have properties scattered around Houston; space precludes listing every one. If you have a favorite "brand," call its toll-free number and ask about Houston accommodations. Again, select on the basis of location, not cost. Houston is a tough city to move around in.

And sometimes it's a tough city to rent a pillow in. Hotel space is extremely tight in Houston during the annual Offshore Technology Conference the first week of May and the Houston Livestock Show and Rodeo the last week of February and the first week of March. During these periods or when three or more conventions are in town, the Greater Houston Convention and Visitors Council (see the *Tourist Information* section below) can tell you which hotels are heavily booked with groups, coventioneers, etc., so you can try elsewhere. When you do call for a room during peak occupancy periods, stress to the hotel that you are *not* in town for a convention.

Super Deluxe

Four Seasons Hotel, Houston Center. 1300 Lamar (Downtown) (77010); 650-1300; 800–268–6282. Occupying one full block in the new 33-block Houston Center redevelopment area downtown, this is without a doubt the finest hotel in a fine hotel town. Fresh yet ageless, spacious yet intimate, Four Seasons seems like the home you always knew you would create if only you had money. The lobby and rooms have wade-through carpeting, the three-story staircase would serve a queen's entrance, and even the elevator is a refined elegance in its own alcove. Amenities include video games in the indoor recreation area, but it's hard to imagine children in this environment. Then again, it may be the rare civilizing influence that makes a difference—bring on the rascals. The fourth floor is a small resort in the city's concrete heart, centered on a year-round heated swimming pool, sun deck, and large whirlpool. Garden rooms overlook this area. The remaining 391 guest rooms are pages from *House Beautiful*—custom-made furniture, fine linens, fresh flowers, bay windows. Guest robes and French-milled soap are included, along with complimentary downtown transportation, overnight shoeshines, in-house movies, concierge and turn-down service, etc. The concern for the guest is incredible—the maid even turns the shower head to the wall on her twice-daily calls. Guests have courtesy privileges at the adjacent Houston Center Athletic Club at a nominal charge, and there are several excellent restaurants on the premises.

Inn on The Park. 4 Riverway (Woodway, just west of the 610 loop) (77056); 871-8181. When a hotel spends $12,000 a month to fly fresh flowers in from Amsterdam, you know quality counts. Beautifully situated in its own park complete with lake and swans, this Four Seasons operation is lovely and hard to leave. Among the surprises: underwater stereo music in the dual swimming pools and some of the more innovative nouvelle cuisine in town in its restaurants. The public rooms are appointed with fine furniture and lavish bouquets, and the 383 guest rooms have the quality linens, marble baths, and the other extras common to Four Seasons operations. Amenities include a fully equipped health club with whirlpool and sauna; jogging trails; concierge service; and courtesy limo transportation to the nearby Post Oak Airline Terminal and Magic Circle–Galleria shopping. The only thorn on this rose of hotels is the limited and inconvenient self-parking. For the nonce, play the role to the hilt and indulge in the valet parking.

The Remington on Post Oak Park. 1919 Briar Oaks Lane (inside the 610 loop near the Galleria) (77027); 840–7600, (800) 392–4659 inside Texas, (800) 231–9802 outside Texas. This 12-story hotel developed by the Rosewood Corporation and the Caroline Hunt Trust Estate of Dallas is on a private three-acre site inside the loop and facing Post Oak Park. Access to Briar Oaks Lane entrance is from San Felipe. This hotel was designed for the upper limits of the carriage trade: The service personnel are dressed by Ralph Lauren, the 248 rooms were developed at a cost of $200,000 each, and the suites run to such niceties as 7-ft. marble whirlpool baths, baby grand pianos, and formal dining rooms for eight. Service is all-important here—the staff will know your name and park your car, the maid will turn down your bed, and the businessman's center will provide dictation and secretarial services via telephone to your room.

The Westin Galleria. 5060 W. Alabama (Galleria) (77056); 960-8100 or (800) 228-3000. One of two Westin hotels that anchor wings of the Galleria, this 495-room hotel is tops in amenities and service. A new in-your-room-dining feature literally brings formal restaurant service upstairs, and some of the bedrooms convert to living rooms, courtesy of beds that fold into the walls. There is also a concierge in the lobby plus complimentary shuttle service to the Post Oak Air Terminal.

The Westin Oaks. 5011 Westheimer (Galleria) (77056); 623-4300, (800) 228-3000. This handsome hotel serves the corporate traveler and tourist, whereas groups and convention business tend to stay at the Westin Galleria, down the mall. In addition to direct access to the shops, skating rink, and major department stores of the Galleria, the Oaks is glowing with a $1.7 million refurbishing that created two executive floors for VIPs, with more to come. Most of the frills, such as concierge, pool, and complimentary transportation to the Post Oak Air Terminal, are standard here. The Roof, atop the hotel, is a Houston favorite for cocktails and free buffet during happy hour and for Sunday brunch. The view and romantic mood are the best in town.

Deluxe

The Doubletree at Allen Center. 400 Dallas (Downtown) (77002), 759-0202; 800-528-0444. Originally the Hotel Meridien, some French flair remains in this sleek 350-room hotel. Guests have a genteel check-in, seated at a small reception desk, and the concierge is outstanding. The Restaurant, however, now features inventive American dishes, not the French cuisine. Good place to stay on weekends when downtown is hopping with one of its major festivals; Sam Houston Park is across the street.

Guest Quarters–Galleria West. 5353 Westheimer (Galleria) (77056); 961-9000 or (800) 424-2900. All luxury suites here, one- and two-bedroom, plus dining areas, fully equipped kitchens, and 24-hour room service. There is also a fine restaurant, a swimming pool, and guest memberships with free transportation at the Houston City Club's all-sports facility. The complimentary transportation covers a two-mile radius of the Galleria location. Transportation to the Med Center can be arranged.

Hotel Inter-Continental Houston. 5150 Westheimer (Galleria) (77056); 961-1500; 800-392-5477 in TX; 800-231-6058 outside TX; 800-327-0200 worldwide. This sleek hotel is the Inter-Continental chain's debut into the highly competitive Houston luxury-hotel market—so expect the best. On the western edge of the Magic Circle area at the intersection of Westheimer and Sage, this three-building contemporary has 518 rooms in two high-rise towers; a heated indoor-outdoor pool; full-scale health club with sauna, massage, whirlpool, and exercise rooms; lighted tennis court; and three racquetball courts. The guest rooms have oversized beds, in-house movies, and bathroom telephones and television. Parking for more than 500 cars is available.

The Houstonian Hotel and Conference Center. 111 N. Post Oak Lane (Galleria) (77024); 680-2626, (800) 392-0784 inside Texas, (800) 231-2759 outside

Texas. Nestled in a 22-acre pocket of forest near the 610 loop west and Galleria, this in-city resort has 247 quiet and well-appointed rooms, plus guests have access to indoor and outdoor running tracks, an Olympic-size swimming pool (usually set up for lap swimming), and assorted courts for tennis, racquetball, volleyball, handball, etc. One of the 10 top spas in the country, the Phoenix (for women only) is on the premises; ask if special programs are open to hotel guests. Also here: a preventive medicine center (680–3330) that will evaluate your personal health and prescribe an intensive exercise and nutrition program. The complete ($530–620) physical takes half a day. If all of the above sounds too serious, you can loll by the inn's second pool or stroll through the woods that isolate this excellent facility.

Hyatt-Regency Houston. 1200 Louisiana St. (downtown) (77002); 654-1234, (800) 228-9000. The tomorrow hotel in the tomorrow city when it was opened in 1972, the Hyatt still holds its own in the downtown area, as much for its eateries and central location as for its outstanding design and accommodations. The 350-foot-high atrium lobby with its zipping glass elevators makes you feel like a movable piece inside a Mondrian painting. The 958 guest rooms have oversized beds and are well-appointed. The 29th floor is the Regency Club, terribly exclusive, with full concierge service and discreet privacy. The sixth floor has 18 lanai rooms with private patios adjacent to the swimming-pool terrace. More than $250,000 worth of original art is scattered here and there, and a full-time horticulturist tends the flora.

The Lancaster. 701 Texas Ave. (downtown) (77002); 228-9500, (800) 392–5566 inside Texas, (800) 231–0336 outside Texas. An $18-million-dollar facelift has turned the old Auditorium Hotel into the elegant Lancaster. The location, directly across from both the Alley Theatre and Jones Hall, is ideal for culture hounds or downtown-bound businessmen. The amenities class it with the elegant small hotels of Europe. The 93 guest rooms have fine furniture, marble baths, fresh flowers, and original art, and the services include a multilingual staff, full-time concierge, in-house valet, etc. Although thick terry towels and complimentary bathrobes are no surprise, this may be the only hotel in town to provide umbrellas, bath scales, and four telephones in every room.

The Lincoln Hotel Post Oak. 2001 Post Oak Blvd. (in the Galleria area) (77056); 961–9300. Designed by I. M. Pei and completed in late 1982 at a cost of more than $70 million, this property is making a high-stakes bid to become one of the world's great hotels. The location can't hurt—just off the 610 loop in the heart of the Magic Circle—and the amenities follow suit. There are multilingual 24-hour concierge service, a soaring atrium lobby humanized with thick rugs and antiques, a garden deck with pool and sauna, and complimentary transportation within the neighborhood. The 455 rooms come with either contemporary or traditional furnishings; just state your preference when you reserve. Security is assured with Uniqey, which reprograms the room door lock with each new occupant.

Stouffer's Greenway Plaza Hotel. 6 Greenway Plaza East (77046); 629-1200, (800) HOTELS-1. Sparkling from a $5.5 million renovation, this high-rise hotel in Greenway Plaza has 389 sound-proof rooms with walk-in closets, dressing rooms, turn-down service, complimentary shoe shines, plus coffee and the morning paper that come with your wake-up call. There's an outdoor pool and whirlpool, plus a health club on the premises. Guests can also use a nearby indoor tennis-jogging-racquetball facility, and there's free transportation to the Galleria, Med Center, and nearby airline terminal.

The Warwick. 5701 Main (77251); 526–1991 or (800) 231–5701. Refurbished by Texas oilman John W. Mecom and family in the 1960s, this sumptuous 310-room hotel reigns like a dowager queen in the Hermann Park–Rice University–Medical Center area south of town. Aubusson tapestries, Baccarat chandeliers, and an outstanding collection of European antiques and art fill the public rooms, with service to match. The upper-floor guest rooms offer some of the best views in town, and the Sunday brunch is a Houston tradition. Med Center transportation via complimentary limo.

Expensive

Adam's Mark. 2900 Briarpark at Westheimer (far west Houston) (77042); 978-7400 or (800) 231-5858. One of the best hotels in the city's western hinterlands, this contemporary house borrows architecturally from the Hyatts, with its 10-story atrium lobby, glass elevators, cushy cocktail-lounge area, etc. Big pluses: an indoor-outdoor swimming pool, fine furnishings in the 604 rooms, and an in-house health club. Guests have privileges at the nearby Westchase Athletic Club, and there's shopping in the huge Carillon Shopping Village flanking the hotel.

The Doubletree Hotel. 15747 Drummet Blvd. (North Belt-Intercontinental area) (77032); 442-8000, (800) 528-0444. Considered by a national rating service one of the three top airport hotels in the country, this 315-room hotel sits on 10 wooded acres and has courtesy transportation to Intercontinental Airport, 5 min. away. Rooms are of residential quality, soundproof, and they have good security. A swimming pool with whirlpool-spa sits in a shady courtyard, and there's golf at the nearby World Houston course.

Holiday Inn–Crowne Plaza Galleria. 2222 West Loop South (Galleria) (77027); 961–7272, (800) HOLIDAY. This $60-million, 501-room hotel has won awards for its contemporary decor. Guests find a relatively inexpensive but luxurious comfort here, including one private floor that includes a concierge, happy hour, continental breakfast, honor bar, and personal secretary in the room rate. All guests can enjoy the free self-parking; sauna, whirlpool, and indoor swimming pool; and the complimentary limo service within the Galleria area.

Holiday Inn–Crowne Plaza. 14703 Park Row (east of the TX 6/I-10 interchange) (77079); 558–5580, (800) HOLIDAY. This second entry in the luxury sweepstakes is ideal for those needing a far west Houston/Park 10 locale.

Hotel Luxeford. 1400 Old Spanish Trail (Medical Center) (77054); 796–1000, (800) 662–3232. This 191-suite hotel has to be the best bargain in town. All accommodations have kitchenettes with microwaves, and the deluxe suites have whirlpool baths. A large Continental breakfast is comp as are local calls, overnight shoe shines, and access to a complete fitness center. A courtesy bus provides free transportation within the area and medical center.

L'Hotel Sofitel. 425 North Beltway, at Imperial Valley Dr. (North Belt–Intercontinental area) (77060); 445-9000 or (800) 231-4612. The emphasis on quality food and wine in its three restaurants, plus a take-out bakery, shows the French touch at this fine 337-room hotel. Even the checkout comes with a complimentary loaf of French bread. The rooms are well furnished and have a small sitting area, and there are a concierge, turn-down service, outdoor pool with bar and whirlpool, indoor pool and sauna, and new fitness club with exercise equipment as well as complimentary transportation to the airport.

Hyatt Regency West Houston. 13210 Katy Freeway (Eldridge exit; far west Houston) (77079); 558-1234, (800) 228-9000. This elegant newcomer has six five-story buildings connected by a large garden atrium, part of the Woodcreek development that includes Conoco and Shell facilities. A lake wanders through the hotel and grounds. There's an outdoor heated swimming pool, whirlpool, health club, two tennis courts, and two restaurants. Maps show running trails nearby, plus there's complimentary transport to nearby shopping centers and golf course. Free self-parking and scheduled airport-hotel transportation ($10).

Sheraton Crown Hotel. 15700 Drummet Blvd. (North Belt–Intercontinental area) (77032); 442-5100 or (800) 325-3535. There's a resort atmosphere here, thanks to the indoor and outdoor swimming pools, game room, health spa, whirlpool, and lively bars and restaurants (two of each). The 439 rooms are comfortable and well done, and there's complimentary transportation to the airport, Greenspoint Mall, and nearby golf and tennis.

The Woodlands Inn Resort and Conference Center. 2301 N. Millbend Dr., the Woodlands (north of Houston in southern Montgomery County) (77380); 367–1100, 800–533–3052 in TX; 800–433–2624 elsewhere. Surrounded by three superb golf courses in the woods 27 mi. north of Houston via I–45, this 268-room lodge and resort is in a world of its own. In addition to challenging golf, the facilities include extensive men's and women's health clubs, a beauty spa, tennis, bicycle rentals, swimming, jogging trails, and one of the nicest swimming pools in the greater Houston area. Ideal when you want to mix pleasure with business in the far north reaches of Harris County. Intercont. airport van ($15).

The Hobby Airport Hilton. 8181 Airport Blvd. (Southeast Houston, within sight of Hobby Airport) (77061); 645-3000 or (800) 445-8667. Southwestern flavor two blocks east of Hobby Airport. A new nine-story tower, plus a three-story cabaña section around the pool. Of the 310 rooms, 30 have separate sitting areas and nine have in-room hot tub–whirlpools. Courtesy transportation to the airport and nearby shopping.

Sheraton Houston Place Hotel. 6800 Main (Medical Center area) (77030); 528–7744; 800–392–4068 in TX; 800–231–0238 elsewhere. Bright and fresh, this 280-room hotel is popular with overnight corporate travelers as well as short- or long-term visitors to the nearby Med Center. More than 200 multiroom suites have fully equipped kitchens and king-sized beds. The complimentary shuttle makes stops at a supermarket as well as Galleria and Sharpstown Shopping Centers, the Med Center and the South Main Air Terminal. Also here: swimming pool, game room, restaurant and bar, free parking, plus a cheerful staff and quality housekeeping.

Note: Reserve at the following Marriott hotels by calling (800) 228–9290.

Marriott at the Astrodome. 2100 S. Braeswood at Greenbriar (77030); 797-9000. Motel-style rooms in a garden setting south of downtown and the Medical Center, near the Astrodome and Astroworld.

Marriott Brookhollow. 3000 North Loop West (T. C. Jester exit) (77092); 688-0100. Adjacent to the Brookhollow business park and across from Northwest Mall in northwest Houston, this 10-story contemporary hotel has "double doubles," oversized beds, or parlor rooms (where the bed folds into a cabinet). There is also a swimming pool and sauna, plus complimentary transportation to the Galleria, Northwest Mall, and the Post Oak Airline Terminal.

Marriott Hotel–by the Galleria. 1750 West Loop South (San Felipe exit) (77027); 960-0111. This contemporary high-rise is a good value for Magic Circle hotels. Comfortable rooms with cable television in each, movies, plus indoor pool, outdoor sundeck, sauna, game room, and free parking in the attached garage. Free shuttle to Post Oak Airport Terminal and Galleria shopping.

Marriott Hotel at Houston Intercontinental Airport. 18700 Kennedy Blvd. (77032); 443-2310. Tucked between terminals B and C, this was formerly the Host International. Now freshened up, the rooms are comfortable and soundproof, and the rooftop restaurant shows off just how much of Houston's land remains undeveloped. Swimming pool, plus intra-airport transportation by tunnel train.

Marriott at the Medical Center. 6580 Fannin (77030); 796–0080. Newly opened, this 398-room hotel has complimentary van service within the health complex, indoor pool and whirlpool, and access to the fitness center at the Institute of Preventive Medicine next door.

Marriott Northbelt. 255 North Belt East (Greenspoint–Intercontinental Airport area) (77060); 875–4000. In the heart of the North Belt business district, this new high-rise has comfortable rooms, indoor-outdoor swimthrough pool with sundeck, whirlpool spa, sauna, and exercise room for working off those stresses. A free shuttle serves the airport and nearby Greenspoint Mall.

Nassau Bay Hilton. 3000 NASA Road One (Nassau Bay/Clear Lake area) (77058); 333–9300. Sparkling new, this 14-story contemporary hotel is very convenient to the Johnson Space Center and has its own marina on Clear Lake. Boat rentals are next door, and there's an outdoor pool with spa, plus a nightclub on the premises. The 244 rooms all have oversized beds and views of the lake.

Wyndham Hotel Greenspoint. 16701 Greenspoint Dr. (North Belt) (77060–1902); 875–2222; (800) 822–4200. Taking sharp aim at the corporate business and meetings trade, this luxury highrise hotel has a 46-foot atrium lobby topped by two large skylights, plus a recreation area and outdoor pool. Guests also have the use of an exclusive athletic club nearby, plus comp van transportation to Intercontinental Airport.

Wyndham Hotel Travis Center. 6633 Travis at Southgate (Medical Center) (77030); 524–6633, (800) 822–4200. All of the 145 suites and 40 king-bedded rooms at this new hotel have wet bars and refrigerators, plus guests have free access to an extensive in-house health club that includes an outdoor jogging track, spas, saunas, etc. There's a dietician on staff and free transportation within the medical center area.

Moderate

Astro Village–Holiday Inn. 8500 Kirby (near the Astro complex) (77054); 799–1050; 800–465–4329. No surprises, in the south part of town.

Astro Village Hotel Complex. 2350 South Loop West (610 South and Kirby) (77054); 748–3221, (800) 392–5398 in Texas, (800) 231–2360 outside Texas. The man who brought the world the Astrodome also created this hotel, complete with the most extravagant and expensive suite in the world stretched across the top floor. This Celestial Suite goes for $3,700 a night and has 13 rooms, ranging from the circus and Tarzan rooms to an opulent master bedroom. The standard guest rooms in this hotel-motel are comfortable but unremarkable, the nicest are around the pool and garden. Great south-of-town location within sight and a long walk of the Astrodome and Astroworld.

Brookhollow Hilton. 2404 North Loop West (T. C. Jester exit) (77092); 688–7711 800–445–8667. Comfortable accommodations and an excellent seafood restaurant, The Anchorage, near the northwest corner of the 610 loop.

Embassy Suites. 9090 Southwest Freeway, Gessner exit (far southwest Houston–Baybrook area) (77074); 995-0123 or (800) EMBASSY. Ideal for families, all 243 rooms are one-bedroom suites with two oversized beds, sitting rooms, and fully equipped galley kitchens. All face into an inner atrium courtyard. Complimentary cocktails in the late afternoon and breakfast in the morning are served in the Mexican-style patio and are included in the room price, as is use of the indoor pool, sauna, and whirlpool.

Hilton Inn West. 12401 Katy Freeway (I–10 West) (77079); 496–9090; 800–445–8667. A good choice if you need housing in the Dairy-Ashford area of far west Houston.

Holiday Inn–Downtown. 801 Calhoun (77002); 659–2222; 800–465–4329. Lots of freebies here: covered parking, in-room movies, and transportation to the Med Center, to the Galleria, and throughout downtown based on availability. When the sun shines between the skyscrapers, you can get a tan around the outdoor pool.

Quality Inn–Intercontinental Airport. 6115 Will Clayton Parkway. (77205); 446–9131, or (800) 228–5151. In the woods east of the airport and midway to Humble and U.S. 59. Comfortable rooms, some with steam baths and whirlpools. Courtesy satellite television, tennis, swimming, and transportation to the airport.

Ramada Inn–Northwest Crossing. 12801 Northwest Freeway (U.S. 290 northwest of 610 loop) (77040); 462–9977, or (800) 2–RAMADA. Excellent accommodations in the city's newest business area. Some rooms have private spas and whirlpools.

Ramada Hotel—Southwest/Sharpstown. 6855 Southwest Freeway (Bellaire Blvd. exit) (77074); 771–0641 or the 800 number above. Comfortable and convenient to the southwest part of Houston.

Sheraton Kings Inn. 1301 NASA Blvd. (Nassau Bay–Clear Lake area) (77058); 488–0220 or (800) 325–3535. Central to the area and to the Johnson Space Center.

Sheraton Town & Country. 910 West Belt (77024); 467–6411 or (800) 325–3535. Well located at West Belt and the Katy Freeway (I–10) on the corner of an expanding shopping center with Neiman-Marcus, Marshall Field, and more than 100 other stores. The top-floor suites are nice, and 32 other rooms open on to the outdoor swimming pool. Helicopter service to Intercontinental Airport is nearby, or bus shuttle to both airports is available (fee).

Westchase Hilton and Towers. 9999 Westheimer (far west Houston) (77042); 974–1000 or (800) 445–8667. Primarily a corporate hotel serving the southwestern and far western business districts. The 308 rooms are large and well-furnished, with complimentary in-room movies. The two top floors have VIP concierge service, complete with the *Wall Street Journal* at your door, and Continental breakfast. Also here: pool, hot tub, and guest memberships at both the Fondren Tennis and Westchase Athletic clubs. Also helicopter service via Airlink Airways (see the *How to Get Around* section below).

Inexpensive

Allen Park Inn. 2121 Allen Parkway (77019); 521–9321, (800) 392–1499 (in Texas), (800) 231–6310 (outside Texas). Comfortable rooms in the near-downtown area, plus a sauna-whirlpool and exercise room.

Comfort Inn–NASA. 1001 NASA Road One (77598); 332–4581. Just east of the I–45 interchange and convenient to the Johnson Space Center–Nassau Bay area.

The Grant. 8200 S. Main (77025); 668–8000. Clean and comfortable with extra-long beds, this small motel is close to the Astrodome and on the bus route to the Med Center. Swimming pool and playground, plus free Continental breakfast.

Harvest House Hotel. 7901 Southwest Freeway (Gessner exit from U.S. 59 South) (77074); 777–2389. Near the Sharpstown area.

Hobby Regency Motor Hotel. 6161 Gulf Freeway (Griggs exit from I–45 South) (77023); 928–2871 or (800) 892–8100. Comfortable accommodations near Gulfgate.

La Quinta Motor Inns. Eleven locations around Houston. Call 800–531–5900 for specifics.

The Bed and Breakfast Society of Houston. 921 Heights Blvd. (77008); 868–4654.

The following offer suites with kitchens, maid service, and other amenities in the Galleria area:

Galleria Oaks Corporate Inn. 5151 Richmond (77056); 629–7120.

Galleria Place Executive Inn. 4723 West Alabama (77027); 621–2797.

Oakwood Apartments. 2424 S. Voss, Suite A101 (77057); 783–4651.

In addition to many lodgings already listed, the following are convenient to the Texas Medical Center. Though not luxury or expensive properties, they offer long-term rates and/or family plans, and free transportation within that district.

The Chief Motel. 9000 S. Main (77025); 666–4151.

Holiday Inn–Medical Center. 6701 S. Main (77030); 797–1110.
Medical Center Visitor's Lodge. 1025 Swanson (77030); 790–1617.
Surrey House Motor Hotel. 8330 S. Main (77025); 667–9261.
Tides II Motor Inn. 6700 S. Main (P.O. Box 25006, 77005); 522–2811.
Special note: **The Ronald McDonald House,** 1550 La Concha (797–0411), provides a residential setting for families of children under 19 years of age being treated at the Medical Center for cancer or other life-threatening diseases. In addition to a community kitchen, laundry, and recreation facilities, there are 21 bedrooms, each of which will sleep four comfortably and six maximum. The room rate is based on the family's income but will not exceed $15 per room per night.
TraveLodge Towers at Greenway Plaza. 2828 Southwest Freeway (Kirby Dr. exit) (77098); 526–4571 or (800) 255–3050. Pleasant accommodations, all with oversized beds. Convenient to Greenway Plaza, Bellaire, and the Rice University area.
The *Westin Oaks* and *Westin Galleria* provide accommodations at no cost on a space available basis to cancer patients and their families while they are receiving treatment on an ambulatory basis. For information, ask your local chapter of the American Cancer Society to contact the reservations department of the Westin Oaks Hotel, 623–4300.

 HOW TO GET AROUND. Unless you know the city well, you will need a good map and a lot of patience, and it helps if you understand the local names for some of the major freeways. When someone talks about the Katy or the Katy Freeway, they mean I–10 west of town (it parallels the Katy Railroad tracks, hence the name). I–10 east of downtown is called the East Freeway. Don't confuse that with the Eastex Freeway, which is U.S. 59 North. U.S. 59 South (from downtown) is called the Southwest Freeway. North of downtown, I–45 is called the North or Dallas Freeway, and south of town it is called the Gulf Freeway. A portion of U.S. 290 West is known as the Northwest Freeway. Few if any of those names appear on the official highway signs, so you'll have to make some mental translations when getting verbal directions.
The confusion multiplies into an Abbott and Costello "Who's on First?" joke when it comes to I–610, better known as the 610 loop, which circles the city. Be prepared to hear "North Loop East," "South Loop West," etc. The first direction refers to the road in relationship to downtown Houston; for example, the north loop is I–610 north of town. The second direction is generally a post-office address used for mailing purposes and has no value to someone trying to find a specific place. Always ask which exit you should use and which direction you should then travel on the frontage road.
From the airport. *Airport Express* provides shuttle service between Intercontinental and the four in-town passenger terminals ($7.50 one way; 523–8888). *Hobby Limousine Service* shuttles passengers between Hobby and four area depots ($5 one way; 644–8359). Call for schedules to the various terminals: Downtown (at the Hyatt Regency on Polk St.); 7011 South Main at Holcombe;

Post Oak, 5000 Richmond (just outside the 610 Loop); and Greenway Plaza, 3769 Southwest Freeway (south frontage road, across from the Summit and between the Wesleyan and Edloe exits).

Airlink Airways operates one air-conditioned Aerospatiale A-Star helicopter between both Intercontinental and Hobby airports and four locations: Transco Tower in Galleria; the Westchase Hilton; Park 10 (I–10 and TX–6 in far West Houston); and downtown at Crawford and McKinney. Reservations advised: 975–8989.

By bus. The *Metropolitan Transit Authority* (Metro) operates a citywide bus system at a modest fare of 60¢, slightly more if you ride a special express route. Although comfort and efficiency are improving, the buses do not serve all the places you'll want to go. You'll need a car if you intend to explore beyond your lodgings. For getting around downtown, there are the Texas Special Red and Texas Special Blue buses. These are marked with red, white, and blue flags and require an exact 25–cent fare. For more bus information, stop at 403 Louisiana in the Hogg Building downtown or call 635–4000.

By car. Unfortunately, Houston's growth has not been accompanied by an equal expansion of the highway system, either in areas served or in car capacity. You can count on stop-and-go traffic from 7:00 to 8:30 A.M. and 3:30 to 6:00 P.M. weekdays, whether inbound to or outbound from downtown. Visitors should be aware that both the Katy Freeway (I–10 west of downtown) and the North Freeway (I–45 north of downtown) have controlled transitways in the center median that can be used only by authorized van pools and buses. Construction delays should be expected. These restricted lanes are clearly posted and closed to general traffic.

Nor do the surface roads offer much relief. Both Houston and surrounding Harris County have developed area by area, without much attention to a comprehensive overall road system or construction for anticipated growth. There are very few limited-access surface roads connecting the various parts of town, and roads engineered to handle local traffic two generations ago are now being pressed into service as major arterials. Streets stop and then start up again miles away, and such niceties as freeway-access signs on the surface streets are rare. Allow twice the amount of time a trip should take based on its actual mileage.

Once on the road, it's every driver for himself, particularly on the freeways. Newcomers often feel that Houston is still the raw hell-bent-for-leather West but that the cowboys have traded in their ponies for pickup trucks. Unfortunately, courtesy on the road is rare, and defensive driving is highly recommended.

On-street parking is limited, and illegally parked cars are towed away and impounded until fines and storage charges are paid. It's best to use one of the many public garages. Rates are generally reasonable, and the covered parking helps handle Houston's weather.

Rental cars. Most of the major car-rental companies are well represented, both at various hotels and service locations in town and at or near the airports. Rates and conditions of rental vary widely. Do some preliminary investigating via the toll-free reservation numbers listed in your local telephone directory, or see a travel agent. Above all, *do not arrive in town without a rental-car reservation* or you may be stranded without wheels.

By taxi. Many taxi companies operate in and around the city. Although they are permitted to cruise and can be hailed from the street, most are lined up outside the major hotels and at the airports. Rates are uniform: $2.45 for the first mile, $1.05 for each additional mile. A ride into town from Intercontinental should be about $24, to the Galleria about $28. There is an additional $1 charge per person from Intercontinental. From Hobby, approximate fares are $13 to downtown, $12 to the Astrodome, and $17 to the Galleria. Cabs can be hailed on the street or called, and you'll find taxi lines at most of the major hotels. Inquire about share-a-ride programs which can cut costs for multiple passengers. Liberty Cab Co., 695–6700; Sky Jack Cab Co., 523–6080; United Cab Co., 654–4040; and Yellow Cab, 236–1111 are among the major firms.

By limousine. More than a dozen rental services provide classy chauffeured transport. A list is available from the Greater Houston Convention and Visitors Council. (See the *Tourist Information* section, below).

By helicopter. Because of Houston's choking traffic, this is becoming an increasingly popular means of getting around. Check with *Airlink Airways*, 975–8989, for schedule.

 TOURIST INFORMATION. The *Greater Houston Convention and Visitors Council* (GHCVC) publishes free maps and is an excellent source of multilingual brochures on local attractions, accommodations, downtown walking tours, shopping, restaurants and entertainment, and general public information. They also prepare a monthly *Day and Night* calendar with detailed information on all sports, theatrical events, and special events going on in the city and surrounding area.

Most of the brochures are available at the information kiosks in the three airport terminals, and the *Day and Night* folder is widely distributed by restaurants, hotels, and businesses throughout the city. All are available by advance mail from the Greater Houston Convention and Visitors Council, 3300 S. Main, Houston, TX 77002. There is also a drive-up information booth with a multilingual staff at that location. Open Monday through Friday, 8:30 A.M. to 5:00 P.M.; Saturday, 9:00 A.M. to 3:00 P.M.; 523–5050, (800) 392–7722 (in Texas), (800) 231–7799 (outside Texas).

Unfortunately, neither of the airports is as well organized. If you need assistance at Houston Intercontinental, search out one of the white paging telephones. Multilingual operators can advise on directions, general information, police or medical assistance, or lost and found. For help at Hobby, check with airline personnel.

Another source of help is *Traveler's Aid,* a United Way agency with volunteers at all three airports and at the main headquarters at 2630 Westridge. If the airport staff is unavailable, call 668–0911 for emergency help 24 hours a day, seven days a week.

The *USO* provides local recreation facilities, programs, and services for active-duty members of the armed forces; 443–2451.

If you are thinking of making Houston your home or are planning an extended stay, contact Community Information Service, 229–9195, for advice on non-profit organizations and government agencies involved in recreation, medical services, legal aid, employment, and a wide variety of social services.

Emergencies have a way of cropping up, even during vacations. Here are a few numbers you may need: Poison Control Center, 654–1701; Emergency Dental Service (after 5 P.M.), 847–7233; Dental Center, 975–9336, 222–2517, and 623–4540; and Galleria Clinic, 961–4050. The following emergency rooms are equipped to handle medical or surgical emergencies around the clock seven days a week: St. Joseph's Hospital, 1919 La Branch (downtown), 757–1000, ext. 1495; Twelve Oaks Hospital, 4200 Portsmouth (off U.S. 59 South), 623–2500. Four others are within the Medical Center complex: Ben Taub General Hospital, 1502 Ben Taub Loop, 791–7300; Hermann Hospital, 1203 Ross Sterling, 797–4060; St. Luke's Episcopal, 6720 Bertner, 791–2121; and Texas Children's Hospital, 6621 Fannin, 791–2222. The universal emergency number, 911, is in operation in Houston.

During your stay the following numbers may be handy: local weather, 529–4444; national weather, 228–8703; road conditions throughout Texas, 869–4571; time, 875–8585. For either police or fire assistance, call 911.

Banks are generally open Monday through Friday from 7:30 A.M. to 5:30 P.M. International currency can be exchanged at the Texas Foreign Exchange Co., 1130 Travis, Monday through Friday, 8:30 A.M. to 6 P.M., and they'll quote the current rate of exchange by telephone; 654–0999. Terminals A, B, and C at Intercontinental Airport have foreign-exchange kiosks, at least one of which is open daily from 7:00 A.M. to 11:00 P.M.; 443–0070. However, they may limit the amount of the transaction because of limited monies on hand.

Houston is one of the few cities in America with high-quality resident companies in opera, symphony, and ballet, as well as professional teams in the major sports. On any given evening, something is going on somewhere in town, from soccer to little theater, from symphony to rodeo. Game and performance information is published monthly by the GHCVC and the *Texas Monthly,* and daily by the *Houston Post* and the *Houston Chronicle.*

There are several ticket sources. *Teletron* (526–1709) gives telephone information and accepts charges on Visa or Mastercard 9:00 A.M.–9:00 P.M., Monday through Saturday, and noon to 6 P.M. on Sunday. The *Astrodome* ticket office (799–9555) is open weekdays 9:00 A.M.–5:00 P.M.. *Ticketron* (526–6557) has outlets throughout the city including *Foley's* department stores. *Houston Ticket Center* (227–ARTS) is in both *Jones Hall* and *Wortham Center* (9:30 A.M. to 5:30 P.M., weekdays; 10 A.M. to 5 P.M. Saturday). The *Downtown Ticket Center* (1100 Milam; 222–8380) sells tickets to movies, sporting events, opera, ballet, symphony, concerts, roadshows, and Gray Line tours. A new *SHOWTIX* booth sells advance tickets as well as half-price day-of-performance tickets in Tranquillity Square downtown (522–9292); open Tuesday–Saturday, 11 A.M.–5:30 P.M.

The Ticket Center, 965–0161, sells choice seats for everything from rock concerts to baseball, and is a good source when all others fail. They offer free delivery weekdays in the downtown and Galleria areas. *Front Row* (977–5555) is another ticket source.

 SEASONAL EVENTS. January. The *International Boat, Sport, and Travel Show* draws crowds to the Astrohall, and feline lovers head for the *Houston Charity Cat Show* at the Albert Thomas Convention and Exhibit Center downtown. This vast facility fills again at the end of the month with a major antique show and sale sponsored by the *Houston Antique Dealers Association* (HADA), one of the best shows of its kind in America. The Houston Tennaco Marathon draws runners from around the world.

February The Astrodome-Astrohall complex is the site of the city's biggest annual shindig, the *Houston Livestock Show and Rodeo.* This kicks off "Go Texan" celebrations all over town. Traffic stops as trailriders come in from outlying areas, camp in Memorial Park, and then parade through downtown. Everyone wears western duds during the 14 days of rodeo and livestock competition, and major national entertainers are part of every evening's show.

March brings a blaze of floral color across the city, the most beautiful of which can be viewed on the annual *Azalea Trail* through the River Oaks–Tanglewood residential area. The grounds of *Bayou Bend* (see the *Museums* section, below) are always part of this two-weekend show. This month also brings the first of the *wildflowers* along the roadsides and the Houston International Festival, a two-week celebration of the arts that features dancers, singers, artists, and musicians in various indoor/outdoor venues throughout downtown.

April marks the *Houston International Film Festival,* which brings famous stars, directors, and producers to town, and the *Doug Sanders Celebrity Classic Golf Tournament* mixes seniors golf with famous names from Hollywood and Nashville.

On **May** 5, *Cinco de Mayo* celebrations show off the city's strong Mexican-American spirit, and in midmonth the *International Gem & Mineral Show* makes the Astrohall glitter.

Warm **June** evenings herald the first of a summer series of ballet, music, and play performances in Miller Outdoor Theatre in Hermann Park. One of these, the *Juneteenth Blues Festival,* is a major party for the city's black community, a musical celebration of the delivery of the Emancipation Proclamation in Texas.

July brings an *Old Fashioned Fourth Celebration* to Sam Houston Park, followed by fireworks there and at various other spots around town.

The Astroworld series of *dog shows* in Astrohall at the end of the month ushers in the infamous "dog days" of **August,** and the following weekend pooches are usually replaced by pistols as the *Houston Gun Collectors* move in with their special exhibition. Meanwhile, back in Hermann Park, the best of the Bard struts the stage of Miller Theatre during the annual *Shakespeare Festival.*

September brings national and jazz musicians to the *Annual Houston Jazz Festival* in Miller Theatre. This is also *British Festival* month, and there is a special arts-and-crafts show complete with bagpipes in Old Market Square.

A *Greek Festival* and *German Oktoberfest* get equal billing in **October,** along with two special day trips out of town. The *Texas Prison Rodeo* at Huntsville is a go-for-broke show unequaled in America, and the *Renaissance Festival* in the woods north of Magnolia re-creates the sounds, sights, food, and fun of the sixteenth century.

If you can't leave town, you'll find the Albert Thomas Exhibit Hall brimming with the elegance of the *Theta Charity Antique Show* and the 100 to 1000 blocks of Westheimer closed to traffic for another swinging *arts festival.*

Early **November** brings *Houston Camper Show* to the Albert Thomas, and then things quiet down until Foley's Annual *Thanksgiving Day Parade* through the heart of downtown. The following Sunday *Santa* arrives at Sharpstown, along with 17 tons of real snow.

The wonderful old homes in Sam Houston Park glow with *candlelight tours* in early **December,** and the world's largest *office party,* free and open to the public, swings at the Galleria a few days before Christmas. The **Bluebonnet Bowl,** a clash of collegiate football teams in the Astrodome, closes out the year on December 31.

 TOURS. Several firms offer commercial tours of the city, NASA, and Galveston—a good way to get your bearings and some historical insight. Among them are: *Tours, Inc.* (530–7506), which uses Mercedes or limos with multilingual operators, and *Unlimited Tours, Inc.,* (694–1519), which covers everything from NASA ($15) to dinner at Shanghai Red's ($35).

Angel's Travel & Tour, 988–0648, offers a variety of tours for Japanese and Chinese tourists only.

Grayline Tours of Houston, 223–8800, has seven tours, multilingual guides, and free pickup upon request at major hotels. Choices include a 4½-hour tour of the city's highlights ($20, including admission to the Astrodome); a 4½-hour tour of NASA ($20); and, Tuesdays and Thursdays, a 7½-hour tour of Galveston ($35 including admissions). For groups of 20 or more, there are charters to Gilley's, the San Jacinto Battleground and Port of Houston, San Antonio, and a working cattle ranch in Hungerford, west of Houston.

Japan Tours & Travel, 520–8654, shows off the Houston area with guides fluent in Japanese, Korean, and Chinese.

Penfeathers Tours, 445–1187, offers weekend birdwatching trips to specific habitats throughout the south coast area. Cost is $20, plus lunch at a local restaurant, and pickup can be arranged. Call for specific details. Houston is on or near two major flyways and offers rich territory for birders.

Three limousine services offer private guided tours on a per-hour basis, usually with a 3-hour minimum: Limousines of Houston, Inc., 699–1444; Limousine Service International, 524–8468; and Royal Limousines, Inc., 928–5544.

There also are some special local tours:

Sam Houston Park has guided tours of four old homes, a church, and an 1824 log cabin, all within the shadow of contemporary skyscrapers and I–45 downtown. Open Monday through Saturday, 10:00 A.M. to 4:00 P.M. (last tour at 3:00 P.M.); Sunday, 2:00 to 5:00 P.M. Adult admission is $2; children 12 to 17, 50¢; children under 12, 35¢; 223–8367.

The Astrodome, the first indoor stadium in America, has tours that include a multimedia presentation at 11:00 A.M. and 1:00 and 3:00 P.M., daily unless there is a game ($2.75 admission, $3 parking; kids under 7 free), 799–9500.

The Lyndon B. Johnson Space Center, better known as NASA, is 20 mi. south of Houston via I–45. Tours are self-guided, beginning at Rocket Park alongside the parking lot and continuing through museum buildings. Sign up for Mission Control Center briefing at the Information desk, Bldg. Two; 483–4321.

The Port of Houston has a free 90-minute narrated tour aboard the M-V *Sam Houston* that is well worth the three-month wait for reservations. If you just drop in, you can view port activity from the observation platform on Kirby Drive, open daily, 9:00 A.M. to 5:00 P.M. Boat tours are at 10:00 A.M. and 2:30 P.M., Tuesday, Wednesday, Friday, and Saturday; 2:30 P.M., Thursday and Sunday. For information and reservations, write the Port of Houston at P.O. Box 2562 (77001) or call 225–4044.

Free van tours of the *Texas Medical Center,* including a 35-min. orientation film, are given Monday through Friday at 10:00 A.M. Reservations should be made at least two days in advance; 790–1136.

The new paddlewheeler *Island Queen* churns away daily from its Brady Island dock (near Shanghai Red's restaurant) on tours of the Port of Houston and up Buffalo Bayou to Allen's Landing, downtown. Sightseeing, dinner, and cocktail cruises are available. For reservations and information, call 868–5323.

Out of Town. A number of regional businesses and industries welcome visitors with a sincere interest in that specific field. For information, contact the GHCVC (see the *Tourist Information* section, above).

The *Taylor-Stevenson Ranch,* 670–1102, welcomes guests by appointment to its vast operation four miles south of the Astrodome. Ideal for families and children, the 2-hour tours are $5 per person. Black-owned and operated for more than a century, the ranch is devoted to preserving black cowboy history and culture.

The city also is surrounded by varied agriculture, and free tours can be arranged through rice and soybean farms, dairy farms, and cattle ranches. For information and reservations, contact the Texas Agricultural Extension Service, 2 Abercrombie Dr. (77084); 855–5600.

Persons with specific interests in cattle raising can request advance reservations to tour the 500–acre *J. D. Hudgins Ranch,* 55 miles west of Houston. A Hudgins bull was the 1984 Houston Livestock Show International Grand Champion. P.O. Box 145, Hungerford 77448; (409) 532–1352.

PARKS. Hermann Park's 545 acres are southwest of downtown via Main and Fannin Sts. Surrounded by class—an 18-hole public golf course on the east, the Medical Center on the south, Rice University on the west, and the Warwick Hotel and Mecom Fountain on the north—this is the city's in-town playground. Scattered around the fringes of the park you'll find the *Museum of Natural Science* and the adjacent *Burke Baker Planetarium;* the *Houston Zoological Gardens;* the *Hermann Park Garden Center* with its special plantings of roses and camellias, and a fragrance garden for the blind; the *Miller Outdoor Theatre;* and the *Houston Belt and Terminal Railway Co.* kiddie train that chugs along a 2-mi. track through the park and woods.

For simple relaxing there are numerous picnic sites and shelters, children's playgrounds, and grassy fields shaded by huge oaks. A large cast-bronze statue of Sam Houston stands at the northwest corner of the park—Sam's hand points toward San Jacinto, where his Texan army won the republic's independence from Mexico in 1836—and a newly refurbished reflecting pool and landscaping fronts the zoo.

For the blessing of **Memorial Park** west of downtown, thanks go to Will Hogg. In addition to the Midas touch, he must have had second sight. One of the movers and shakers of Houston in the early 1900s, Will Hogg developed the city's most elegant residential area, River Oaks, in 1924. Then, perhaps foreseeing the unplanned, unzoned, mercilessly concrete development that is today's Houston, he donated 1,000 acres of virgin woodland to the city with the stipulation that if it was ever used for anything but park purposes, it would revert to the Hogg estate. An additional 500 acres was later purchased, and today Memorial Park not only commemorates those who lost their lives in the First World War, but it also adds quality to life in Houston.

In addition to a challenging public golf course, Memorial Park includes a tennis center, jogging-hiking-biking-exercise trails, polo grounds, an archery range, picnic areas, and the wilderness along Buffalo Bayou that is the *Houston Arboretum and Nature Center.*

Sam Houston Park, bounded by Bagby, McKinney, and Dallas Sts. downtown, preserves a handful of the city's historical structures in a small, rolling green. The only building on its original site is the *Kellum-Noble House* (1847), the oldest brick house in the city. The *Nichols-Rice-Cherry House* (1850) was once the home of William Marsh Rice, founder of Rice Institute (which later became Rice University). *St. John's Church* (1891), the *San Felipe Cottage* (1875), the *Pillot House* (1868), and the *Old Place* (1824) are scattered around the park. The new *Gallery of Texas History* museum shows artifacts from 1519 to the present time, including the "Come and Take It Cannon" and salvage from 16th-century shipwrecks off the gulf coast. Self-guiding and free, the museum is open 10:00 A.M.–4:00 P.M., Monday through Saturday; 1:00–5:00 P.M., Sunday.

Entrance to the park is open and free, but tickets for guided tours and access to the buildings are available in the *Yesteryear Shop* in the Long Row, which fronts on Bagby. The *Tea Room* serves great soup/salad/sandwich lunches Monday through Friday, 11:00 A.M. to 1:30 P.M. You can either eat inside, outside on the spacious patio created by the new museum, or pack it all up for a picnic outdoors in the park, one of downtown's unsung pleasures. For more information, call the Harris County Heritage Society at 655–1912.

Two blocks north on Bagby, **Tranquillity Park** tops an underground parking garage with a Bicentennial tribute to the Apollo flights. An intricate walk-through fountain with waterfalls and reflecting pools forms the heart of the park, and assorted grassy knolls represent the earth, lunar mounds, and other celestial bodies. Bronze plaques at the entrances tell the Apollo story in 15 languages, and a replica of Neil Armstrong's footprint on the moon is a good search-and-find project for children. The best time to visit is late afternoon, when the angle of the sun can turn the fountain into a shower of golden light.

While you're in the neighborhood, jog across Walker to **Martha Hermann Square,** which surrounds the reflecting pool in front of Houston City Hall. If you can't find a hotel room, not to worry. You can legally sleep here undisturbed by the law (no guarantees about other problems). That was a stipulation of George Hermann when he gave this pocket park to the city in honor of his mother some years ago.

A long green corridor of grass, trails, and playgrounds called the **Allen Parkway Recreation Area** borders Buffalo Bayou and Allen Parkway immediately west of downtown. Access is from Allen Parkway or Memorial Drive, but don't go alone any time or linger after dark.

For a look at Houston as it was before the Allen Brothers began their real-estate promotion, journey south of town via I–45 and then east on Bay Area Blvd. to the **Armand Bayou Nature Center.** This park and wilderness center preserves plant and animal life in its natural habitat. In addition to free explorations of the estuary by pontoon boat, you can follow nature trails or explore by canoe. For information, call 474–2551. For boat ride reservations, call the Bay Area County Park System, 326–6539, weekdays only.

ZOO. Alas, there is only one, officially known as the **Houston Zoological Gardens but generally just called the Hermann Park Zoo.** One of the few major zoos in the country that is free, it includes among its many pleasures an excellent children's petting zoo, an unusual nocturnal-animals exhibit, a walk-through aviary, and the new Kipp Aquarium. If you have children in tow, bring some bread or crackers to feed the ducks in the pond outside the zoo, and save some time to ride the train (80¢). Both the zoo and the train are open daily, year-round, but the hours change with the season. During the summer they are 9:30 A.M. to 8:00 P.M. Parking is free. Note: an admission fee may be charged. Information: 523–5888.

GARDENS. The 155-acre **Houston Arboretum and Nature Center** is on the western edge of Memorial Park, a towering buffer of native East Texas trees within a toot of traffic on the 610 loop. Yet when you walk the more than 5 mi. of trails, civilization seems very far away. Guided tours are given on

Sunday afternoons whenever a small group forms, and self-guiding maps are available daily in the headquarters building. Buffalo Bayou is au naturel here, so the mosquitos can be fierce—come prepared. Free and open daily, year-round. Information: 681–8433. From the west loop (610) take the Woodway exit and turn east toward downtown.

More than 200 species of plants native to Texas thrive at a vest-pocket arboretum and natural-science museum in the Spring Branch area, the **R. A. Vines Environmental Science Center,** 8856 Westview; 465–9628. Another 17 acres bordering Rummel Creek in the Memorial area forms the **Edith Moore Sanctuary,** operated by the Houston Audubon Society. There's good access from the northwest corner of the parking lot of Memorial Drive Methodist Church, 12955 Memorial Dr., or from the sanctuary entrance at 440 Wilchester. Information: 932–1392.

The gardens of **Bayou Bend** are beautiful and open to the public any time of the year (see the *Museums* section, below). In the spring, this is one of the most comprehensive showcases in the South for azaleas. Rose and camellia growers will find much of interest in the test gardens of the **Houston Garden Center,** 1500 Hermann Dr. in Hermann Park; 529–5371.

Several commercial nurseries offer interesting looks at Houston's tropical flora. *Condon Gardens,* 1214 Augusta inside the west loop (I–610), specializes in specimen plants laid out in garden fashion, a delight just to visit. Information: 782–3992. Three other noteworthy gardens lie some distances from town: *Lilypons Water Gardens,* just south of I–10 on FM 1489 in Brookshire (36 mi. west of downtown Houston), specializes in water lilies, lotus plants, etc., including the fauna to make your water garden come alive. Best of all, you pick and they mail, even the goldfish: 934–8525. An hour's drive north of Houston via U.S. 59 and assorted country roads, the *Hilltop Herb Farm* occupies a fragrant corner of the Sam Houston National Forest west of Cleveland. The local gurus on herbs, their use, and their culture, owners Madeline Hill and Gwen Barclay give tours. For information, write Box 1734, Cleveland, TX 77327; 592–5859. *Lowrey Nursery,* in southern Montgomery County near the Woodlands, is the prime source of native plants in South Texas. Directions: 367–4076.

 CHILDREN'S ACTIVITIES. Astroworld and **Waterworld** top the lists. Adjacent to the south loop (I–610) east of Kirby Drive and across from the Astrodome, both are part of the Six Flags chain. Astroworld has more than 80 rides and several stage shows for the $15.95 admission price. Waiting areas are covered and air conditioned. Open Tuesday through Sunday from Memorial Day through Labor Day, weekends in spring and fall. Waterworld is 15 acres of wet family fun. Open daily June through August, weekends only in May and September. Admission is $11.50; 799–1234.

Children's Museum, 3201 Allen Parkway, encourages exploration of technology, the arts, and other cultures with many hands-on play areas. A mini-supermarket lets them shop, handle money, and play grocer. Open Tuesday through Sunday; 52–AMUSE.

Fame City, a $40-million amusement park, opened in mid-1986 at 13700 Beechnut in far southwest Houston, 1 mile northeast of TX–6. It offers fun for all ages, including bowling, miniature golf, movies, video arcade, eateries, a treasure island inside a 25-acre air-conditioned building, and everything from a wave pool to inner-tube slide in a 10-acre outdoor facility called Water Works. Children 8 and older can be dropped off; those younger must be accompanied by an adult. The indoor facility is pay-as-you-use with no basic admission charge and is open daily, year-round. Water Works is $10.95 for adults; $8.95 for children 42 inches tall and under; and free to children under two and adults over 55. The swimming facility is open daily in summer, weekends only in May and September–December.

Houston Police Museum (17000 Aldine Westfield Road; 230–2300) and the **Houston Fire Museum** (2403 Milam; 524–2526) are fascinating for children. Both are open daily, and admission is free.

Splashtown USA (21300 I–45 North in Spring; 350–4848) is a 30–acre water theme park that entertains with a 500,000-gallon wave pool called Big Surf, Shotgun Falls, the Zoom Floom, and nine other twisting and turning coolers. There's also a kiddie pool, ball crawls, and net climbs for the toddler set. There are more than 50 lifeguards and EMS specialists on duty at all times, and rafts, tubes, and water sleds are free with the admission price. There also are Friday night dances for teens, and families are welcome to bring their lunches and coolers and picnic on the grounds. Open Wednesday through Sunday, May through September. $11.95 for adults; $8.95 children over two years and under 46 inches.

Nathan's Physical Whimsical, inside the Sharpstown Mall (Southwest Freeway at Bellaire), is an indoor fun park with more than 20 rides and activities aimed at developing children's motor skills. Open daily; no smoking allowed. $4.26 for children, $1 for adults; 777–5437.

Rodeos are a Texas tradition that children love. During the summer the Future Farmers of America Club of Cy-Fair High School stages the **Cy-Fair Rodeo** every Friday night on Telge Road, just off U.S. 290 West in the northwest section of Harris County. For information: 373–0530 (Cy-Fair High School). The sagging Houston economy has temporarily closed the Round-Up Rodeo in Simonton, 36 mi. west of Houston via FM 1093 (Westheimer). When it reopens, expect a lot of action in the standard rodeo events, plus a calf-and-goat scramble for kids—you may even go home with a live souvenir of Houston. This indoor facility is air-conditioned, and an optional inexpensive barbecue dinner is served before the show. Call to check on their current status, 346–1534.

The downtown area has several free delights for children. Just walking through the soaring lobby of the Hyatt Regency Hotel or riding its glass-enclosed elevators (one looks onto the lobby; the other, out onto Houston) is thrilling to the young. From the Hyatt it's easy to move into the labyrinths of the underground tunnel system. There's an ice-cream parlor hidden in there somewhere—follow the directional maps.

Just outside the west loop (I–610) the Galleria offers hour of exploring fun—kids love the souvenir and magic stores on the lower level of Galleria

I—and ice skating at the Ice Capades Chalet; 626–1292. Older children thrive on a double-header science trip south of town to **NASA/Johnson Space Center** (see the *Museums* section, below), combined with a stop at **Armand Bayou** (see the *Tours* section, above) or a visit to the **Robert A. Vines Environmental Science Center,** an ecology-teaching facility of the Spring Branch School District (see the *Gardens* section, above). For children's theater see the *Stage* section, below.

PARTICIPANT SPORTS. From fall to early spring, Houston's generally mild weather allows a variety of outdoor sports without much regard for the seasons. Summer's heat and humidity, however, can be overwhelming, particularly between 10:00 A.M. and 4:00 P.M. From mid-April through September, it is wise to hunt up an air-conditioned indoor facility or settle for some form of water recreation.

Although *runners* and *joggers* seem to sprout among the cars on many city streets, most folks run on trails along the bayous or in the parks. Special Exertrails combining a jogging course with exercise stations begin at the garden center in Hermann Park and at the tennis center in Memorial Park. There are similar Exertrails along Brays Bayou (on South Braeswood, between Stella Link and Buffalo Speedway in southwest Houston) and in MacGregor Park, 5225 Calhoun (southeast of downtown).

An extensive system of *hike-and-bike trails* links many of the bayous, parks, and business centers. Free detailed maps are available from the Houston Parks and Recreation Dept., 2999 S. Wayside (77023); 641–7530; *Bicycles* can be rented from several of the U-Haul Centers in town. Check the phone book for nearby locations and call. Serious 10-speeders will enjoy the Alkek Velodrome, an indoor banked track at Cullen Park, off Barker–Cypress Road in West Houston (578–8511).

For a general listing of all current sport races and tournaments check the "Thursday Weekend Preview" section of the *Houston Chronicle* or the weekend section of the Friday *Houston Post.* The Sunday papers usually include an additional rundown on things to do.

Seventeen *golf* courses are open for public play in the greater Houston area. Check with the most popular regarding specific location, fees, tee times: Bear Creek Golf Course, 859–8188; Brock Park Course, 458–1350; Glenbrook Park Golf Course, 644–4081; Gus Wortham Park Golf Course, 921–3227; Hermann Park Golf Course, 529–9788; Melrose Park Golf Center, 667–8887; Memorial Park Golf Course, 862–4033; Sharpstown Park Golf Course, 988–2099; World Houston Golf Club, 449–8384; and Stephen F. Austin State Park Golf Course, (409) 885–3613.

Although many private stables offer boarding and training, only a few offer *horseback riding* by the hour. Try *Avis Rent-a-Horse,* 497–1630, or *White Acres Stables,* 568–0254.

Swimmers have their choice of 47 municipal pools operated by the city parks and recreation department. Not all are in "good areas," so caution is advised. For information: 641–7509.

The city parks-and-recreation department also operates three major *tennis* centers with outdoor laykold courts, shops, showers, instruction, etc. The Homer Ford Tennis Center is southeast of downtown at 5225 Calhoun, 747–5466; the Memorial Drive Tennis Center is west of downtown at 1500 Memorial Loop Dr. in Memorial Park, 861–3765; and the Southwest Tennis Center is at 9506 S. Gessner, 772–0296. More than 80 public courts in various stages of repair are scattered around town.

If either *swimming* or *tennis* is a major sport for you, a best bet in Houston would be to look for a hotel that includes those recreations in its offerings.

Though opportunities are limited, *canoeing* is growing in popularity in Houston. Organized *float trips* to various bayous and creeks in the greater Houston area and to the Guadalupe, Rio Grande, and Medina Rivers can be arranged through several outfitters: Texas Canoe Trails, (512) 625–3375; River Safari, Inc., 528–2800; Guadalupe Canoe Livery, (512) 885–4671 or (512) 964–3189; and Whitewater Experience, 522–2848.

Locally, you can canoe on Buffalo, Armand, and Dickinson Bayous and both sail and canoe on Clear Lake. Rentals are available from River Safari, Inc., 528–2800 and Whitewater Experience, 522–2848.

Windsurfing is another popular water sport, particularly in Galveston Bay and on Clear Lake. Check those last numbers given for rentals or call South Coast Wind Sports, 660–9915. T-Marina, 61st St. and Offats Bayou in Galveston (409–744–9031) has rentals for windsurfing, water-skiing, sailing on small boats and catamarans, and paddleboating.

Although there are catfish in the bayous that thread through Greater Houston, serious *fishing* means a trip to Clear Lake and Galveston Bay or out into the Gulf. Information on marinas, charter party boats, etc., is available from the Clear Lake Area Convention & Visitors Bureau, 1202 NASA Road One (77058); (488–7676), and from the Galveston Convention and Visitors Bureau, 2106 Seawall Blvd., Galveston, TX 77550; (409) 763–4311; 800–351–4236 in TX; 800–351–4237 elsewhere. Galveston Party Boats (bay and gulf fishing) has a toll-free Houston number: 222–7025.

Both Lake Livingston and Lake Conroe north of Houston are known for their bass fishing. For a list of marinas and facilities on Lake Conroe, contact the Conroe Visitor & Convention Bureau, P.O. Box 2347, Conroe (77305); (409) 756–6644. For Lake Livingston, contact the Polk County Chamber of Commerce, 516 W. Church St., Livingston (77351); (409) 327–4929.

The fastest-growing sport in America is *racquetball,* and three Houston health clubs are open to guests: Continental Racquetball (in the 1960 area), 893–5146; Courts West Racquetball Club (Bear Creek area), 463–6815; and the Westchase Racquetball and Athletic Club (southwest), 977–4804.

SPECTATOR SPORTS. When the tides of fortune are running high for one of the city's three major professional-sport teams, it's standing room only at the games. When the *Houston Oilers* lost their NFL Super Bowl bid in the playoffs in 1980, they were welcomed home with a party that filled the Astrodome and spilled out into the parking lots. Good thing they didn't win—it would have immobilized the city.

The Astrodome is also home to the *Houston Astros* baseball team and the *Houston Rockets* play NBA basketball at the Summit in Greenway Plaza.

On the collegiate level, most of the major schools field high-quality teams in all three sports, but football is king in Texas and draws the most emotion. For who is playing whom where, when you're in town, check the papers and call the school directly or call Ticketron (see the *Tourist Information* section, above). And don't pass up a chance to see a swim meet at the natatorium of the University of Houston, which has one of the best teams in the country year after year.

Celebrity tennis tournaments pop up several times a year at some swanky places, and both soccer and rugby are played on a non-pro basis on area fields. Professional wrestling is a year-round draw at the Coliseum downtown, and horse-racing fans can ride special buses east to Delta Downs in Vinton, Louisiana, for a day of playing the ponies; (800) 551–7142.

HISTORIC SITES. In addition to Allen's Landing and Sam Houston Park in the downtown area, there are several historical sites well worth a day's trip.

San Jacinto Battleground State Historic Park, 22 mi. southeast of downtown via TX 225 and technically in La Porte, marks the site where a ragged band of Texans led by Sam Houston defeated the mighty Mexican army led by Santa Anna and won independence for Texas in 1836. The 570-ft.-high San Jacinto Monument has the stirring story chiseled around its base and an excellent free museum inside (see the *Museums* section, below). The elevator ride to the top of the monument is $2.00 for adults, 50¢ for children. Pick up a free detailed map of the battleground at the museum and then wander among the oaks and old tombstones near the picnic grounds. Nearby, the *U.S.S. Texas* is open for tours daily, year-round ($2.00 adults, $1 children six through 17), and kids love climbing on the gun enplacements that flank this only surviving dreadnought-class battleship. Several picnic areas border the Houston Ship Channel and upper Galveston Bay, ideal for crabbing or bank fishing.

Sam Houston Memorial Park, in Huntsville, 69 mi. north of Houston via I-45, has two historic homes in which Houston lived, his law office, and an excellent museum on Texas history, all free and open daily from 9:00 A.M. to 5:00 P.M., year-round. For information: (409) 295–7824.

Washington-on-the-Brazos State Park, northwest of Hempstead, marks the site of the first constitutional convention that created the Republic of Texas in 1836. None of the original buildings survives, but a replica of Independence Hall has an audio-visual show about the historic times in this tiny town, and the Star of the Republic Museum is a lodestone of Texana. A picket fence surrounds Barrington, home to Anson Jones, the fourth and last president of the Texas Republic. This trip is without equal in early April, when the fields flow away from the park in waves of wildflowers. All the above are open daily, 10:00 A.M. to 5:00 P.M., March through Labor Day; Wednesday through Sunday only the rest of the year. For information: (409) 878–2461. From Houston take U.S. 290 west through Hempstead to Chappell Hill. Turn north on FM 1155 to Washington. Chappell Hill also has several historic homes. Inquire at any of the stores on Main St.

Henkel Square is a collection of early Texas homes and buildings on the square in Round Top, a tiny hamlet in the hills between Houston and Austin. Funded by the Texas Pioneer Arts Foundation, Henkel Square has won national awards for its painstaking restorations, and docents lead visitors on detailed tours. Tickets are $2 for adults, $1 for students, and can be bought in the brightly painted Victorian building that used to be Round Top's drugstore. Open daily, 10:00 A.M. to 5:00 P.M., year-round except major holidays. This is a comfortable two-hour drive from Houston via U.S. 290 West and Texas 237 South. Information: (409) 249–3308.

Winedale is 4 mi. north of Round Top via FM 1457 and FM 2714 and, with careful timing, can be combined with a visit to Henkel Square. Now part of the University of Texas, Winedale is a rural farmstead that functions as a living museum. The two-story Sam Lewis house is furnished to the period and has unusual stenciling and ceiling frescoes. Around it are a smokehouse, a pioneer kitchen, and a barn where University of Texas English-department students perform Shakespeare on August-weekend evenings. In the back pasture is the rather elegant McGregor-Grimm House, a fine example of a pre-Civil War plantation home in cotton-rich Texas. Although Winedale's grounds are free and open daily, the buildings are open only on Saturday from 10:00 A.M. to 6:00 P.M. and on Sunday from noon to 6:00 P.M., with a small admission charge. There are often special events here, so check before you go; (409) 278–3530.

 MUSEUMS. As Houston's cultural consciousness has risen and expanded in the last decade, so have the quality and fortunes of its handful of museums, concentrated primarily in the Hermann Park–Montrose–Rice University area. A day's exploring can mix and match several to suit your personal interests. A listing of current special exhibits and traveling shows is published in numerous magazines and brochures (see the *Tourist Information* section, above).

The Museum of Fine Arts. The original physical core of this somewhat confusing building is a neo-classical rectangle, to which have been added a series of wings and galleries. Entrance is through the Brown Pavilion on Bissonnet, a contemporary horizontal arc of glass that completes an expansion designed by Mies van der Rohe. Pick up a map at the door to keep your bearings as you move through the various areas and exhibits. When you've saturated your appreciation level, the museum's small lunchroom serves some of the best salads and sandwiches in town.

Because much of the money for acquisition and expansion over the years has come from corporate or private philanthropic gifts representing differing motives and tastes, the collection covers a vast range of art history. Of note are the Straus Collection of Renaissance and eighteenth-century works, which includes *Temptation of St. Anthony* by Fra Angelico; the Beck Collection of Impressionist and Postimpressionist paintings by Daumier, van Gogh, Cassatt, Signac, Derain, Braque, Kandinsky, Bonnard, and Matisse; and the Samuel H. Kress collection of Italian and Spanish Renaissance works, among which is Bellotto's *The Marketplace at Pisa.*

At the opposite end of the spectrum are a fine collection of Remingtons; *Number 6, 1949,* by Jackson Pollock; *Two Women Before the Window* by Picasso; and significant oriental, pre-Columbian, African, and Oceanic art. Within the past five years the museum has been aggressively expanding its photography collection, a portion of which can usually be seen in the Lower Brown Mezzanine.

Significant sculpture including works by Calder and Rodin is scattered around the museum's shady backyard (the former front entrance), and a new sculpture garden links the museum with its school, the *Alfred C. Glassell, Jr., School of Art* across Bissonnet. Small exhibits of high-quality student work are usually on display in this second building.

A guide to the entire collection is available in the museum's bookstore, along with a brief list of things you shouldn't leave without seeing. In addition, more than 20 traveling shows open here annually. Parking and Thursday admissions are free. Other days are $2 for adults, $1 for seniors and students. Open Tuesdays, Wednesdays, Fridays, and Saturdays 10:00 A.M. to 5:00 P.M.; Thursdays to 9:00 P.M.; Sundays 12:15 to 6:00 P.M. Try to catch the free 30-min. gallery talks by museum instructors at 1:30 and 2:00 P.M. on Thursday and Friday, year-round. For information: 526–1361.

A third portion of the Museum of Fine Arts, *Bayou Bend,* is across town in the River Oaks residential area. This unusual Latin-Colonial home with its 14 oak-studded acres of gardens along Buffalo Bayou was the former home of one of the museum's great patrons, Miss Ima Hogg. Designed by noted architect John Staub, Bayou Bend was built in 1927 to house Miss Ima's extensive collection of American antiques. She gave both the collection and the home to the Museum of Fine Arts in 1965.

Miss Ima had a discerning eye and bottomless pocketbook, and the collection reflects both. One of the finest museums of its kind in the country, Bayou Bend is open for tours only by advance reservation ($4 for adults, $3 for seniors), and in the spring, there's often a wait of several weeks. If all else fails, the second Sunday of every month except March and August is open house through only the gardens and downstairs rooms, from 1:00 to 5:00 P.M. For information: 529–8773.

The Contemporary Arts Museum. Diagonally across from the Museum of Fine Arts on the corner of Montrose and Bissonnet sits an aluminum-sheathed trapezoid. This is the somewhat "spacey" Houston home of the avant-garde in art, a most curious place. To the uninitiated, it seems the museum carries the "life is art, art is life" theme to new limits. Do drop in and have your art consciousness raised—those in the know say the professional staff is doing an ever-improving job. Open Tuesday through Saturday, 10:00 A.M. to 5:00 P.M.; Sunday, noon to 6:00 P.M. There are free guided tours of the Upper Gallery exhibitions at 2:00 P.M. on Sunday, and the museum's shop has beautiful hand-crafted gifts and inventive toys for children. 526–3129.

A major addition to Houston's art scene opened to international fanfare in mid-1987. The **Menil Collection,** a multimillion-dollar museum designed by Renzo Piano, houses the extensive contemporary and ethnic art collection of Dominique de Menil and family at 1515 Sul Ross in the Montrose district. Open Wednesday to Sunday, 11 A.M. to 7 P.M., 525–9400.

A tiny jewel of a museum, **The Rothko Chapel,** is adjacent at 3900 Yupon at Sul Ross, between the 1300 and 1400 blocks of W. Alabama. Free and open daily from 10:00 A.M. to 6:00 P.M., this is a place to soothe the spirit and lift the heart through peace or meditation. The small octagonal room is lined with 14 huge monochromatic paintings by the late Mark Rothko, and the sculpture in the adjacent park, *Broken Obelisk* by Barnett Newman, comments on the life and sudden death of Martin Luther King. Beautiful in and of itself, this chapel is a good place to pause for more than a moment in your sightseeing. For information: 524–9839.

The University of Houston has two gallery-museums, the **O'Kane Gallery** on the downtown campus (across Buffalo Bayou via N. Main Street from the downtown business district), 221–8042, and the **Blaffer Gallery** on the main campus (entrance 5 off Cullen Blvd.), 749–1329. Both host changing exhibits in a variety of media. Call to see what's up.

Another small museum of interest to Americana fans is the **Museum of American Architecture and Decorative Arts** on the second floor of Moody Library at Houston Baptist University, 7502 Fondren (southwest). Free and open Tuesday through Thursday, 10:00 A.M. to 4:00 P.M.; Sunday, 2:00 to 5:00 P.M. For information: 774–7661, ext. 2311.

Five other museums deal with life as lived rather than as perceived through art. The **San Jacinto Museum of History** is in the base of the monument at San Jacinto Battleground State Historic Park (see the *Historic Sites* section, above). One gallery showcases a permanent collection that follows a time line from pre-Columbian years to the end of the 19th century. The second gallery holds special exhibits. A 5-screen, 56 projector multimedia show on the Texas Revolution is planned. Some 14 paintings by Charles Shaw are in the South Gallery. Free; open daily, 9 A.M. to 6 P.M. For information: 479–2421.

The **Houston Museum of Natural Science, Burke Baker Planetarium,** and the **Museum of Medical Science** share a wooded site at the north end of Hermann Park. One of the largest natural-science museums in the Southwest, the *Houston Museum of Natural Science* has everything from dinosaur skeletons to seashells, including an excellent exhibit of Indian artifacts collected from Alaska to South America. The story of oil is told in clear terms in the Hall of

Petroleum Science and Technology, and important events in Lone Star past come to life in the Strake Hall of Texas History. The main-floor galleries of the new Frensley Wing often showcase important traveling exhibits. Best of all, this is a hands-on place. You are welcome to feel, examine, or manipulate anything that is not behind ropes or glass. For information: 526–4273.

Upstairs, the Harris County Medical Society welcomes you to the *Museum of Medical Science.* "Talking exhibits" explain human anatomy and physiology, and visitors can test their eyes, lung capacity, and heart. Graphic models follow the development of a fetus and the miracle of birth. The remaining life processes are explained by TAM, a transparent/talking mannequin. For information: 529–3766.

The *Burke Baker Planetarium* explores the universe 16 times a week in its computerized theater, and the shows change with the seasons. By advance arrangement you can view the heavens through the 16-in. reflector of the Margaret Root Brown telescope. For information: 526–4273.

All three museums are open Tuesday through Saturday, 9:00 A.M. to 4:45 P.M.; Sunday and Monday, noon to 4:45 P.M. Admission is $2; Thursday mornings are free.

The words "Houston . . . the *Eagle* has landed" not only brought instant international recognition to the city on Buffalo Bayou, but they also announced the age of man in space. The **NASA/Lyndon B. Johnson Space Center,** south of Houston in the Clear Lake–Nassau Bay area, is headquarters for America's space program, and visitors see lunar rocks, rockets and spacecraft, training labs, and other examples of today's space technology.

NASA visits start at Space Park (alongside the parking lot) where three rockets are on display, including a giant four-stage Saturn V. Self-guided tours begin at the Visitor Center (Building 1) and continue through four other facilities; Mission Control Center (sign up for tours at the information desk as soon as you arrive); Mission Simulation and Training (you can walk through skylab and shuttle trainers); the Lunar Sample Building; and the Space Shuttle Orbiter Training. Plan on driving to the last two; it's a long walk. In all, the NASA experience requires about three hours and stamina. NASA is free and open daily except Christmas from 9:00 A.M. to 4:00 P.M. Information: 483–4321.

ART GALLERIES

From old masters to contemporary hand weaving, Houston's commercial art galleries serve a broad audience. Although scattered all over town, the majority are in the west sector, with several in the Galleria alone. Few specialize in any one form of art, but the following list may help you narrow the field to your particular interests. The best bet is to pick up a free magazine, *Art Happenings of Houston,* available at all the museums and galleries and at the guest-information counters of major hotels. Current exhibits are also listed monthly in *Houston City* magazine and *Texas Monthly,* and weekly in the local papers.

Archway Gallery, 2600 Montrose, 522–2409, is a cooperative, exhibiting the better regional artists in all media, including Raku. The *Art League of Houston,*

1953 Montrose Blvd., 523–9530, also covers all media, with excellent juried or invitational shows at various times of the year. *Davis-McClain Galleries,* 2627 Colquitt, 520–9200, exhibits contemporary and traditional realistic landscapes, paper works, and sculptures. *DuBose–Rein Galleries,* 1700 Bissonnet, 526–4916, focuses on contemporary paintings and sculpture and is a favorite with leading interior decorators. *Harris Gallery,* 1100 Bissonnet, 522–9116, showcases the newest of Houston's artists with works on paper, paintings, and photographs. *Hooks-Epstein Galleries,* 3210 Eastside, 522–0718, focuses primarily on late-nineteenth- and early-twentieth-century European works on paper, paintings, and sculpture. *Jack Meier,* 2310 Bissonnet, 526–2983, specializes in contemporary Impressionistic and abstract paintings, watercolors, and sculpture, with emphasis on regional artists. *Kauffman Galleries,* 2702 W. Alabama, 528–4229, handles new works in all media, from photography and lithography to painting and sculpture, by major international contemporary artists. *Meredith Long & Co.,* 2323 San Felipe, 523–6671, handles major contemporary American artists and fine nineteenth- and twentieth-century American paintings. *Moody Gallery,* 2815 Colquitt, 526–9911, represents 15 contemporary regional artists working in painting, sculpture, and other media. *The Watson Gallery,* 3510 Lake at Colquitt, 526–9883, focuses on contemporary paintings and works on paper of young Houston artists. *Houston Center for Photography,* 1435 W. Alabama, 529–4755, is the showcase for area photographers.

 MUSIC. The musical arts thrive in Houston. The mid-1987 opening of the $70-million Gus W. Wortham Theater Center added two new theaters, principally for the use of the Houston Grand Opera and the Houston Ballet. Jones Hall remains the premier auditorium for the Houston Symphony and the Houston Pops Orchestra, and numerous musicals and stage shows play at the Music Hall. All are in the downtown Civic Center/theater complex, as is the Nina Vance Alley Theater. Tight stage space finds many productions moving to *Wortham Theatre* on the University of Houston's central campus year-round or to *Miller Theatre's* outdoor stage during the warm months. For current offerings, check the local newspapers, magazines, etc., as noted in the *Tourist Information* section, above.

The *Houston Symphony Orchestra,* currently under the baton of Sergiu Comissiona, presents a full season of concerts from September through May in Jones Hall, often with internationally acclaimed artists in guest roles. During the summer the symphony presents a special Summer Festival and evening outdoor concerts in Miller Theatre in Hermann Park. For information: 227–ARTS.

Symphony musicians also present six Pops weekend programs with guest conductors in the Music Hall, and a series of chamber orchestra and chamber music concerts are offered on an intermittent basis throughout the September–May season. For information on either, call 224–4240.

Popular music in a symphonic context is also the theme of the *Houston Pops Orchestra,* conducted by Ned Battista in six to eight performances annually, in either Jones Hall or the Music Hall. This is the only year-round pops orchestra in the world, and the second half of their concert "season" usually features internationally known guest artists such as Dinah Shore, Pearl Bailey, and José Greco. Information: 871–8300. *Texas Chamber Orchestra* performs chamber-orchestra and ensemble music in an eight-concert series at St. John the Divine Episcopal Church, 2450 River Oaks Blvd. It sponsors some Saturday afternoon children's concerts at various locations around town. For tickets and information, call 529–5744.

Chamber music is also performed by the *Shepherd School of Music at Rice University*, 527–4933; the *University of Houston Central Campus Music Ensemble*, 749–1116; and *Music America*, 376–2525. Some musicians within those groups specialize in baroque and Renaissance music of the twelfth through seventeenth centuries, as do the *Cambiata Soloists*, 488–1928 or 667–6351.

A variety of music is performed year-round at *Festival Hill in Round Top*. Founded and directed by noted pianist James Dick, the Festival Hill programs are usually performed by guest artists either on an outdoor stage under the stars of the rural Texas countryside or in the new air-conditioned Festival Concert Hall. The April-to-August series is more intimate, often chamber music played in the parlors of the handsome old William Lockhart Clayton house. Gourmet dinners and overnight accommodations can (and must) be arranged in advance; (409) 249–3129. Picnickers are welcome; be aware that there is only one small cafe in Round Top. Ask directions when you call and plan on a two-hour drive from downtown Houston to get there.

Music for love, not money, motivates the 70-member *Houston Civic Symphony* to give six free weekend concerts annually, often in the Brown Auditorium of the Museum of Fine Arts. Guest artists add to programs ranging from Bach to Stravinsky. For information: 682–6767.

Music lovers should also investigate the Rice University Concerts, 527–4933; the Christ Church Cathedral Concerts, 222–2593; the University of St. Thomas Concerts, 522–7911, ext. 240; and the University of Houston Concerts, 749–3796. The Houston Baptist University School of Music, 995–3338 also performs at various locations in the Houston-Galveston area.

Chances are if a major musical show is playing in Houston, it has been produced either by the Houston Grand Opera (HGO), Theatre Under the Stars (TUTS), or the Society for the Performing Arts.

The *Houston Grand Opera's* season and offerings know no limits in the new Wortham Theater Center. The basic season of seven major operas features internationally known singers in roles ranging from traditional scores of *Turandot* and *Rigoletto* to premieres of innovative works. Don't worry about not understanding what you see, English translations of the original language text are projected by computer onto screens above the stage arch. The same management also produces the Spring Opera Festival at Miller Theater in Hermann Park, coproduces touring shows with other opera companies, and creates fresh shows that open in Houston and then go on the road (*Porgy and Bess, Treemonisha*, etc.). HGO also sponsors the *Texas Opera Theatre* and the *Houston Opera*

Studio, both of which give musical-theater programs or recitals in Houston at various times. HGO information: 227–ARTS or 546–0200.

Theatre Under the Stars presents guest artists and local professional singers in six major light-opera musicals a year, one of which is a free production, each summer in Miller Theatre. The winter season plays in the Music Hall, and TUTS's December production of *Scrooge* has become a Houston holiday tradition. 622–1626 or 622–8887 (box office).

The *Society for the Performing Arts* presents major cultural attractions from around the world in Wortham Theater Center and Jones Hall from September through June. Among their plums are the Houston premieres of both the Pittsburgh Symphony Orchestra and L'Orchestre de Paris conducted by David Barenboim. For information: 227–1111.

Choral music is a Houston specialty all its own. The *Houston Symphony Chorus* (224–4240) gives concerts as well as accompanying the symphony upon occasion, and the *Betty Devine Singers* of Houston present formal concerts several times a year (627–3609). The three universities previously mentioned here also have choral groups; inquire at the numbers given.

The S.P.E.B.S.Q.S.A.—*Society for the Preservation and Encouragement of Barber Shop Quartet Singing in America*—is active here (493–9258), and the local *Gilbert and Sullivan Society* (627–3570) mounts full-stage performances of those favorites every summer.

DANCE. Most major American dance companies perform in Houston, courtesy of the Society of the Performing Arts. The *Houston Ballet,* under the artistic direction of Ben Stevenson, tours throughout America, gaining a strong reputation for its varied repertoire and technical precision. Founded in 1955, it became a professional company in 1969 and presents six programs of six performances each in Wortham Center during its September-through-May season. The company traditionally performs *The Nutcracker* at Christmas. For information: 227–ARTS.

The *City Ballet of Houston,* under the direction of Margo Marshall, performs throughout the year, often showcasing new ballets by local and national choreographers. For information: 468–3670.

Young dancers in training perform with the *Allegro Ballet* (496–4670) in six concerts yearly. The American heritage is the focus of the *Southwest Jazz Ballet Company* (694–6114) in 50 performances each year, and contemporary dance is performed by *Chrysalis Repertory Dance Co.* (528–0031) in Heinen Theatre on the central campus (downtown) of Houston Community College.

STAGE. In theatre lingo, Houston is a great "break a leg" town. One of the three oldest professional resident companies in America, the Alley Theatre, thrives here with a strong playbill year-round except for September and nearly two dozen professional and fine amateur groups compete as smaller satellites.

From a humble first performance in a small room literally at the back of an alley in 1947, the *Alley Theatre* now plays in a multimillion-dollar downtown house that resembles a contemporary castle, with turrets and ramparts. Inside, two shows often run simultaneously, a major production in the 800-seat large theater and a more intimate show in the 300-seat Arena theater. In all, this professional resident company produces 15 shows with 500 performances each year. Downtown businesspeople enjoy the full one-act plays featured at Lunchtime Theatre (12:15 to 1:00 P.M.) during the October-June season and either comedies or mysteries spice up the summer. For the current play and ticket information, call the box office at 228–8421. Tickets bought between 12:00 noon and 1:00 P.M. on day of performance are half-price; a special student rate ($5.00–$6.00) is available 15 minutes prior to curtain. Stand-by tickets are available only when the house is sold out, with seating in any available seat just before the play begins.

The drama department of the University of Houston central campus produces a *Children's Theatre Festival* during July and August in the Wortham Theatre. For information: 749–3459. Children's theater is also the focus of *Theatre on Wheels* (953–1666). In addition, the *Carranza Puppets* (947–0920), and the *Main Street Theatre* (524–6706) often stage productions for the younger set.

Students at the Houston International Theatre School (HITS) perform a two-week *Children's Theatre Jubilee* during the summer, featuring the HITS Unicorn Theatre Company. For information: 861–7408.

Offering plays ranging from the avant-garde and experimental to classics and melodrama are the Country Playhouse, 12802 Queensbury, 467–4497; Main Street Theatre, 2540 Times Blvd., 524–6706; The Ensemble, 3535 S. Main, 520–0055; Stages, Waugh & Allen Parkway, 527–8243; and Theatre Suburbia, 1410 W. 43d, 682–3525.

Also, check what's playing at the *Arena Theatre,* 7326 Southwest Freeway (at Frondren) (777–1212), and at the *Tower Theatre,* 1201 Westheimer (529–5966).

 SHOPPING. Greater Houston, with a population of more than two million people, offers shopping opportunities from probably the most exotic and wildly expensive merchandise in the world to budget items and flea markets. A drive through and around Houston, either on or off the freeways, reveals that one is never more than a few minutes away from a shopping area. These can range from a cluster of four stores on one block to vast full-service shopping centers and malls covering acres.

In the heart of downtown Houston from the 800 to the 1200 blocks on Main St., and on the avenues on either side of it, are department stores and specialty shops. The major department store downtown is *Foley's* on Main, between Lamar and Dallas streets. The store's parking garage is adjacent and is one of the least expensive in the downtown area.

The new Park in Houston Center is the first major retail development to be built in downtown in a generation, a multi-story mall entered from San Jacinto, McKinney, and Lamar streets. From there, you can enter the city's underground tunnel system, much of which is lined with small shops, service businesses, and eateries. You also can enter this four-mile labyrinth from the lobby of the Hyatt Regency Hotel, and from most of the major banks and office buildings. The banks, in particular, supply maps for this weather-controlled shopping-and-eating adventure.

The most famous shopping area in Houston is *The Galleria* at Post Oak and Westheimer. In this L-shaped, three-level structure are two deluxe hotels, an Olympic-size skating rink, five major nationally known specialty stores, four theaters, 19 restaurants, a medical clinic, a private health club, and office facilities. The Galleria is noted for the quality of its stores, which include *Neiman-Marcus, Gumps of San Franciso, Fred Joaillier of Paris, Tiffany & Co., Mark Cross, Alfred Dunhill, Peck & Peck, Charles Jourdan, Ted Lapidus, Au Chocolat, Lord & Taylor, Frost Bros.,* and *Laura Ashley.* This list names but a few of the more than 300 businesses in the Galleria. Of course, you will find less-expensive stores there, with merchandise ranging from books and candles to luggage and cutlery. The Galleria has free parking.

Another shopping sector nearby and teeming with exclusive merchandise is on Post Oak between Westheimer and San Felipe. On Post Oak, facing Westheimer and the Galleria, is the *Sakowitz* Post Oak store, Houston's most famous home-owned specialty shop for men, women, and children. Continuing along Post Oak on the same side of the street, you will come to *Abercrombie & Fitch,* which specializes in imports and items for those who have everything (how does a miniature VW for children, which operates like a full-grown car, at $7,000, grab you?). The sportswear department will send you decked out as the chic-est gal or guy on the block to hunt elephant or shoot ducks.

In the next block is *Saks Fifth Avenue,* with a bevy of shops that surround it in its own miniature Galleria, shops such as *Polo, Pierre Deux, Cartier, Sonia Rykiel,* and *Rive Gauche.* At San Felipe—still on Post Oak—is yet another group of elegant stores that specialize in fine merchandise. But that's not all. On the opposite side of Post Oak are more clusters of boutiques all the way back to Westheimer.

Other shopping areas are sprinkled strategically about Houston. *Greenspoint Mall* is near the Intercontinental Airport at the intersection of I–45 and North Belt. *Deerbrook Mall* is northeast of the airport in Humble; and *Willowbrook Mall* is in northwest Harris County at the intersection of FM–149 and FM–1960.

Other total shopping can be found to the west of Houston at *Town & Country* on the West Belt at Katy Freeway (I–10); *Memorial City* on Gessner and Katy Freeway; *Carillon West, Westwood, Northline Mall,* and *Sharpstown* at Bellaire and US–59. To the south of the city are *Gulfgate, Almeda Mall, Almeda Square,* and *Baybrook Mall.*

At Shepherd Dr. and Gray, the *River Oaks Shopping Center* consists of white and black art-deco buildings that house shops to service the extremely affluent neighborhood with art and antique galleries as well as more mundane shops. Born-to-shop visitors shouldn't miss *Highland Village,* a series of small upscale stores inside the loop in the 4000-4300 blocks of Westheimer. Need solid gold faucets for your bath? Avant-garde designer fashions? This is fertile ground, and a favorite of the ritzy ladies of River Oaks. A turn south from Westheimer on either Bammell or Sackett brings you to a charming collection of Victorian homes known as the *Gardens of Bammell Lane.* Now home to nine boutiques, including the outstanding *Gypsy Savage* (antique frames, dressing table necessities, jewelry), this square-block also has the *Bistro Garden* restaurant (reservations suggested).

The Village, near Rice University and the Medical Center complex, is a bit more than four blocks square, another area offering total shopping. It has more than 500 stores, restaurants, and business establishments in a wide price range. On Rice Blvd. you will find specialty shops selling exclusively British merchandise for example, or Scandinavian, though at 2415 Rice Blvd. you will find the last of the old 5 and 10s, *Variety Fair.* Variety Fair seems not to have stored any of its stock in more than 30 years, so they are bound to have exactly what you need, from Easter grass in July to sand pails in December. The Village is bounded by Rice and University Aves. on the north and south and by Kirby and Greenbriar on the east and west.

If it is flea markets you like, *The Common Market,* at 6116 Southwest Freeway (U.S. 59 South) (782–0391), and *Four Seasons Common Market,* at 4412 North Shepherd (697–4765), should have what you want. If not, try *Trade Mart,* 2121 West Belt North (467–2506), which specializes in antiques, or *Trading Fair II,* 5515 South Loop East (731–1111). Both are air-conditioned and have free parking. A branch of the famous outlet store, *Loehmanns,* 7455 Southwest Freeway (777–0164), offers high-quality merchandise at low prices.

For western wear that is good if not high styled or high priced, try *Stelzig's Western Wear,* 3123 Post Oak, near Richmond in the Galleria area; 629–7779, and on the Southwest Freeway (US–59) at Bissonnet; 988–6530.

Sears, Montgomery Ward, and *Penney's* are in many shopping centers. The White Pages can be helpful. If your eyeglasses need tightening or the car needs fixing, check the Yellow Pages.

Westheimer Road has an artsy area, too: east of the Galleria, between the 100 and the 1900 blocks. Here you can find neon sculpture, unusual cards, old movie posters, T-shirts, candles, leaded glass, paintings, wood and ceramic work, fancy writing paper. At Avondale and Westheimer are six or seven boutiques with the usual abundance of antique and flower shops.

In the Galleria, small, slender men can find imported Italian clothes to fit them at *Copperfield, Leopold Price and Rolle. Norton Ditto* has handsome menswear both downtown and in the Post Oak area. Maternity clothes and bridal attire can be found in specialty shops in almost every shopping center. *James Avery's* gold and silver craftwork is available on Post Oak. Tex-Mex and Texas foods can be found in *Sakowitz* and *Neiman-Marcus.*

Special suggestion: Do not plan to walk from store to store unless you have no streets to cross. Be prepared to move your car to each different shopping area, even if it is nearby. Parking is free, and the traffic is too heavy to deal with on foot.

 DINING OUT. Houston enjoys an abundance of fine restaurants, but it isn't easy to find them. As is everything else in this city, the excellent eateries are widely scattered across more than 550 square miles, and they're often situated in the most unlikely places, since Houston has no zoning. There is nothing to keep your next-door neighbor from tearing down his house and putting up a gas station or, for that matter, a restaurant. So don't be surprised if you stumble across a gourmet dining room in a little bungalow on a residential side street. At the same time, you're just as likely to find such a spot in some seedy strip shopping center, wedged between a grocery and a drugstore. (Many restaurateurs who flocked to Houston during the oil boom like sharks drawn to blood have moved on to other waters. If you visited a couple of years ago, don't necessarily expect your favorite restaurant to still be here.)

Many first-time visitors to Houston assume that the only restaurants worthy of serious consideration are those specializing in barbecue and Mexican food. Well, if a person were to have but one meal here, it would be a shame not to enjoy a plate of smoked brisket or some *tacos al carbón*. But these regional specialties represent only a fraction of Houston's culinary offerings. As the city's sophistication level has risen, so too have the fortunes of the canny restaurateurs who cater to the increasingly demanding tastes (with one eye on the increasingly ample bank accounts) of the local elite. But you needn't be loaded to eat well in Houston. For every high-priced haven of haute cuisine, there are dozens of down-to-earth diners and burger joints, not to mention the ever-growing number of moderately priced dining establishments that turn out consistently fine fare. Additionally, over the past half dozen years, the number of excellent ethnic eateries has burgeoned, imparting a welcome international flair to the local restaurant community. All together, these places are spreading Houston's reputation as a restaurant town. Surely, he who is tired of eating in Houston has simply lost his appetite.

Price classifications and abbreviations. The price ranges given for the listed restaurants are determined by the cost of an average meal for one person, including appetizer, main course with vegetables, and dessert. Drinks, tax, and tip are **not** included in our ranges and will add to your tab. The tax on meals in Houston is 7¼%. An *Inexpensive* designation means a meal should run less than $10; *Moderate,* $10 to $20; *Expensive,* $20 to $30; *Deluxe,* $30 to $40; and *Super Deluxe,* more than $40.

Abbreviations for credit cards are:

AE—American Express
CB—Carte Blanche
DC—Diner's Club
MC—MasterCard
V—Visa

Abbreviations for meal codes are:

B—Breakfast
L—Lunch
D—Dinner

Always call first to double-check hours of operation. Call to reserve at most expensive, deluxe, and super-deluxe places. Check then on the dress code.

AMERICAN ECLECTIC

Expensive

Cafe Annie. 5860 Westheimer (west of Galleria); 780–1522. In the sophisticated surroundings of this strip shopping center restaurant, the menu features unusual combinations and sauces laced with inventive genius and a high respect for the best of fresh food. Quite simply, one of the best chef-owned spots in town. L, Tuesday through Friday; D, Tuesday through Saturday. AE, MC, V, DC.

Charley's 517. 517 Louisiana (Downtown); 224–4438. This upscale upholstered place is popular with expense-account folks heading out for a grand evening in the downtown theater district. Bypass the evening specials and stick with the standard menu. Good choices include the roast rack of lamb or the filet of red snapper, sauteed with Louisiana lump crabmeat and served in a cream sauce. D, Monday through Saturday. All major credit cards.

Confederate House. 4007 Westheimer (Highland Village); 622–1936. Surely this is the best place in Houston to sample that celebrated Texas delicacy, the chicken-fried steak. This method of cooking steak (breaded and deep fried) probably originated as the poor man's answer to Wiener schnitzel and is a time-honored way of camouflaging bad meat in countless roadside cafés. But that's not the case at the Confederate House. Their chicken-fried steak is fabulous, as are all the other steaks at this genteel, clubby restaurant near the exclusive River Oaks neighborhood. Fried shrimp are also noteworthy, as are the onion rings and French fries. The extensive wine list is especially strong on Californias. And be sure to leave room for a wonderful southern-style dessert: pecan fudge balls. L, Monday through Friday; D, daily. All major credit cards.

Rainbow Lodge. 1 Birdsall (near Memorial Park); 861–8666. Despite an eclectic menu ranging from pasta primavera to game birds, the food at this in-town hideaway can't compete with the eccentric decor, which manages to be elaborate and rustic at the same time. With its secluded location and whimsical architecture, the Rainbow Lodge seems right out of some fractured fairy tale—and it's charming. Sit in the glassed-in dining room, order the dependably good sautéed liver, and enjoy your view of the dense woodlands along Buffalo Bayou. You'll never believe you're in the middle of the nation's fourth-largest city. L, Tuesday through Friday; D, Tuesday through Saturday. All major credit cards.

River Oaks Grill. 2630 Westheimer (at Kirby Dr.); 520–1738. No, those stuffed trophy heads were not bagged locally, but they do give a nice hunting-lodge touch to this popular place. The menu ranges through a variety of grilled seafood to some well-handled beef and veal standards. California expatriates love the San Francisco–style sourdough French bread (served hot) and the classic Caesar salad. D, Monday through Saturday. Reservations advised. AE, MC, V.

The Warwick Sunday Brunch. Warwick Hotel, 5701 Main (museum area); 526–1991. Watching people strut their Sunday best at the Warwick has become a Houston tradition, but don't let the local swells distract you from the matter at hand: a glorious monument to culinary excess. Buffet tables bend under the weight of enormous ice sculptures that loom over huge platters of shrimp, oysters, crab claws, pâté, and more salads than anyone could reasonably hope to sample at one sitting. Quite a spread, but go easy—the next room has the cooked-to-order omelets, succulent roast beef, and a dessert table. The rich, dark coffee may be the best in town. Sunday brunch, 11:00 A.M. to 2:30 P.M. All major credit cards.

Moderate to Expensive

Blue Moon. 1010 Banks (Montrose); 523–3773. With owner-chefs as gifted as Yvonne and David Mancini in the kitchen, you are assured of a special dining experience. Where else in town would you find smoked salmon pasta with Vidalia onions and black caviar, or sautéed lamb with sun-dried tomatoes, oyster mushrooms, and champagne sauce and served with polenta? Bonus: This delightful place overlooks a small park by day and has a bar and live jazz club on the second floor by night (grazing menu until 1 A.M.). Sunday brunch ranges from seven-grain apple pancakes with honey butter to four types of Italian frittatas, with other goodies in between. L, Tuesday through Friday; D, Tuesday through Saturday; Brunch, Sunday. AE, MC, V.

Charley T's. 3700 Buffalo Speedway; 960–9711. A grilled veal chop that will melt in your mouth is a recent addition to a fine collection of steaks, shrimp, and chops that has to be rounded off with Charley's famous homemade butterfinger ice cream topped with chocolate sauce. L, Monday through Friday; D, Monday through Saturday. All major credit cards.

Ouisie's Table. 1708 Sunset Blvd. (Rice University area); 528–2264. Ignore the feeling that you've wandered uninvited into a private party and find out why those hordes of casually stylish people continue to jam this trendy spot near the Rice campus. The answer is on the blackboard: the everchanging menu usually includes steak, chicken, lamb, seafood, and a vegetarian dish, but some things are better than others. The real standouts are the cold entrées. L,D, Tuesday through Saturday; AE, MC, V.

Shanghai Red's. 8501 Cypress (on the ship channel); 926–6666. This Rube Goldbergesque restaurant-cum-warehouse in the heart of the city's industrial district may be the ultimate theme restaurant. It's very silly and very, very popular (expect a wait even with reservations). The price may be high for standard "surf 'n' turf " fare, but the real reason to come here is to get a good look at the ship channel. Houston has a closed (fenced) port, so this is about as close as you'll get without signing on for a stint in the Merchant Marine. The view is not pretty, but it does have a certain commercial-industrial charm. L, D, daily. All major credit cards.

Inexpensive to Moderate

Paradise Bar and Grill. 401 McGowan (near downtown); 522–9509. Welcome to paradise. This curious eatery on the southern edge of downtown has the feeling of a renovated speakeasy: dim lighting, no windows, ragtime music. But the best part is the food, which is inventively prepared, invariably fresh, and very reasonably priced. Lunch features deli specialties; dinner specials include the Paradise burger (stuffed with bleu cheese) and chicken Morocco, cooked with yogurt and spices over an open flame. Service is winningly earnest. L, Monday–Friday; D, Thursday–Saturday.

TGI Friday's. 5010 Richmond (Magic Circle), and other locations; 627–3430. Anyone familiar with Manhattan's Upper East Side will recognize this bright blue building near the Galleria as a clone of one of the world's most successful singles bars. Well, one needs nourishment before a night on the prowl, and Friday's fills the bill with a formidable menu. You'll need a speed-reading course if you plan to read the entire menu before ordering. Burgers, potato skins, omelets, and salads are quite good. L, D, daily. All major credit cards.

The Wine Press. 1962 W. Gray (River Oaks); 528–6030. Favored dishes at this quietly elegant little dining room include chicken breast Monterrey, artichoke beef, and fettucine with shrimp and white sauce. The fresh-fruit offerings make a very nice lunch, and as you would expect, they have a wide selection of wines. L, Sunday–Friday; D, daily. AE, MC, V.

Inexpensive

Antone's. 807 Taft (near downtown), and other locations; 526–1046. Exemplary po'-boy sandwiches (sliced loaves of French bread loaded with Italian cold cuts) make this ethnic grocery a popular noon-hour spot with downtown office workers. Take it to go or enjoy it out back in dilapidated "po'-boy park." L, Monday through Friday; open until 6:30 P.M. during the week, 7:00 on Saturdays; hours at other locations may differ. No credit cards.

Becks Prime Drive Thru. 2902 Kirby (River Oaks); 524–7085. The real McCoy old-fashion hamburger joint—seven types of burgers grilled over hickory. The wonderful malts are 10 percent butterfat, with fresh strawberries or Hershey's chocolate mixed in. Best of all, you can call ahead and then just drive through to pick up your order, or you can head for the deck or patio on a nice day. L, D, daily. No credit cards.

Black-eyed Pea. 2048 W. Gray (River Oaks), and other locations; 523–0200. This Dallas-based chain successfully mass produces southern home-style meals. Chow down on meat loaf, chicken-fried steak, fried catfish, and black-eyed peas at any of five locations around town. This food is better than your mama would want to believe. L, D, daily. AE, MC, V.

Chili's. 1952 W. Gray (River Oaks), and other locations; 528–6443. Another down-home sort of place, Chili's is a block or so down the street from the Black-eyed Pea (and, again, at other locations about town). The emphasis here is on burgers and, you guessed it, a bowl of Texas red, with or without beans. As a matter of necessity, the draft beer is very cold. L, D, daily. AE, MC, V.

The Culpepper Burger Company. 802 Lamar (downtown); 654–1144. If you get the hungries for hamburgers, fried chicken, or fajitas while trapped in the canyons of downtown, this is a good choice. There's a full bar, plus you can park free in Foley's garage (with validation) after 5 P.M. If you want to eat on wheels, call ahead; ask about the 10 percent discount on orders to go. B, L, Monday through Friday; D, Monday through Saturday. AE, MC, V.

Frenchy's. 3919 Scott (University of Houston area), and other locations; 748–2233. Despite appearances, this is not just another fast-food outlet. The spicy fried chicken is better than you'd ever imagine and puts the Colonel to shame. Don't bother with the greasy French fries—move right on to the savory beans and rice or the pungent dirty rice (rice cooked with liver). Crumble some corn bread into the bacony mustard greens and enjoy a taste of heaven. L, D, daily. No credit cards.

Fuddrucker's. 3100 Chimney Rock (Magic Circle) and other locations; 780–7080. Yes, it's an ugly name, but they happen to produce the number-one contender for best burger in Houston. The secret just may be the fresh meat. Inside this large tin building (it looks sort of like a gazebo of the Titans) you'll see the glassed-in meat locker housing huge sides of beef about to be ground, grilled, and slapped onto a fresh homemade bun. Help yourself to the lettuce, tomatoes, and other garnishes (avoid the gummy melted-cheese sauce) and enjoy your burger out in the beer garden with an icy longneck. Fuddrucker's also serves steaks, hot dogs, and wurst. And just try to leave without sampling one of those huge brownies. L, D, daily. AE, MC, V.

Goode Company. 4902 Kirby (Rice Village area), and two other locations; 520–9153. Look for fairly standard American fare with a regional twist: burgers, chicken, fajitas, and hot dogs grilled over mesquite. Onion rings and fries, of course. L, D, daily. No credit cards.

Hobbit Hole. 1715 South Shepherd (River Oaks); 528–3418. Vegetarian items dominate the menu at this pleasantly laid-back establishment, though burgers are available for unregenerate carnivores. The colossal egg-salad sandwich, adorned with sprouts, sunflower seeds, avocado, and tomato on whole wheat, is certain to expand your Middle Girth. Other sandwiches are equally memorable, and the iced herb tea is a pleasant alternative to Lipton's. L, D, daily. AE, MC, V.

Longhorn Cafe. 2536 Richmond (Montrose) and other locations; 528–1260. Enjoy chicken-fried steak and other Texas specialties in an airy down-home atmosphere. There's a real fine country-style breakfast that includes the best hash browns in town and big flaky biscuits with cream gravy for dippin'. Just ask for the BDB—Best Deal Breakfast. B, L, D, daily. All major cards.

Luby's. With 17 locations scattered throughout town, this best of all cafeterias is Houston's dining room away from home. The food is tasty and varied, most dinner trays top out at less than $5. Hours vary with locations, so check the telephone book for the nearest one and call. All serve lunch and dinner. No credit cards.

Treebeard's. 315 Travis (Market Square, downtown); 225–2160. If you've never sampled Louisiana red beans and rice, get in line. This airy, cafeteria-style restaurant on Market Square serves up what's probably the best commercial version of this Cajun specialty to be found west of the Sabine River. L, Monday through Friday. AE.

Vie de France. 5085 Westheimer (Galleria II); 840–7227. Tromping around the Galleria for the afternoon can be wearisome. This bakery near Marshall Field turns its fresh French loaves into sumptuous sandwiches that will keep you on your feet for another round of conspicuous consumption. Try the roast beef, or a piece of quiche with soup or salad. The chocolate-and-almond croissants, by the way, are nearly irresistible. L, D, daily. No credit cards.

BARBECUE

Inexpensive

Gabby's. 9401 S. Main (Astrodome area), and other locations; 661–0957. Though Gabby's is a chain operation, the place has the look and feel of an old boardinghouse, which is fine by the patrons here, since the barbecue is a darn sight more acceptable than the victuals turned out by most chain restaurants. Not the best barbecue in town, but it'll do. L, D, daily. AE.

Goode Company. 5109 Kirby (Rice Village); 522–2530. The walls of this chowhouse are so laden with Texana—from steer heads to tractor seats to rodeo posters—that it could damn near double as a junk shop. But the most authentically Texan thing about the place is the constant ching of the cash register. (The taped music places a close second.) Barbecued chicken is the best of the smoked meats here. The beans are the best in town. The pecan pie is the best in the world. That's a fact. L, D, daily. No credit cards.

Green's Almeda Barbecue. 5404 Almeda (near the Medical Center); 528–5501. This is barbecue with soul. While the sausage links may be too greasy for most palates, the ribs are sure to make a true believer out of anyone. For a "light" meal, try the chopped-beef sandwich. It's so greasy—and so good. L, D, Monday through Saturday. No credit cards.

John's Barbecue Stand. 1402 Crockett (near downtown); 223–5671. If Gabby's is masquerading as an old-time barbecue place, this is the real thing. John's has been around so long, some of the regulars even look smoked (you'll recognize them by the brown paper bags they tote in to the back tables). Smoked brisket and links are perfectly respectable here, but the best choice is either the ribs or (even better) the barbecued pork, which is relatively hard to find in Texas. The finely shredded cole slaw is a favorite among many good side dishes. B, L, D, Monday through Friday. No credit cards.

Luling City Market. 4726 Richmond (Magic Circle); 871–1903. Roy Jeffrey cooks *the best* barbecue in Houston right here. Roy learned how to smoke meat at the original Luling City Market in Central Texas, an area that's justly famous for its good barbecue. And now that Roy has forsaken Central Texas, plenty of barbecue-loving Houstonians hope he'll never go home. The ribs are rich and succulent; the mildly spicy links plump and moist; the lean beef brisket a sheer marvel. Ask the cutter to slice you some "outside" beef, the dark brown crusty part. The smoky taste reveals the secret of truly good barbecue—it doesn't need sauce. Nonetheless, you'll find a bottle of Roy's piquant sauce on every table, just in case you care to liven things up a bit. As if all that weren't enough, the beans, cole slaw, and potato salad are exemplars of their kind, there's a full bar, and iced tea refills are free. L, D, Monday through Saturday. AE, MC, V, DC.

Luther's. 1100 Smith (downtown), and other locations; 759-9748. Another good chain operation, Luther's has outlets at half a dozen spots around town serving up your standard Texas-style beef barbecue with all the fixin's. The location near the main library is convenient if you're anywhere downtown. L, D, daily; downtown location closed weekends. MC, V.

Otto's. 5502 Memorial at Reinecke (near Memorial Park); 864-2573. Otto's is a sentimental favorite among Houston barbecue aficionados, but that sentiment is backed up by years of good eating. The brisket is consistently moist and flavorful. Try it sliced on a sandwich with a side order of slaw topped with sliced jalapeños (which you serve yourself)—it's the classic Houston lunch. L, D, Monday through Saturday. No credit cards.

CHINESE

Expensive

Uncle Tai's Hunan Yuan. 1980 Post Oak Blvd. (Magic Circle); 960-8000. There's still a restaurant of the same name on New York's Upper East Side, but Uncle Tai is in the kitchen of his Houston outpost (which is now his headquarters). Since his arrival several years ago, the Uncle has secured his reputation here with such Hunanese specialties as stir-fried duck with young ginger, scallops with garlic sauce, and hot-and-sour fish broth. L, D, daily. All major credit cards.

Moderate to Expensive

Dong Ting. 611 Stuart (downtown); 527-0005. San Hwang, the owner, is perhaps the most engaging host in Houston. His kitchen continues to turn out such delectable dishes as lion's head (crab and pork meatballs) and Hunan peasant's delight, a blissful union of twice-cooked bean curd and pork with green onions. House specialties may be had at lunch for a reduced price, accompanied by hot-and-sour soup or salad, and rice. Peking dust, mingled layers of dried crushed chestnuts and whipped cream, is an ethereal dessert. L, Monday through Friday; D, Monday through Saturday. All major credit cards.

Inexpensive to Moderate

Shanghai East. 5015 Westheimer (Galleria); 627-3682. Another New York transplant, this Szechuan restaurant on the third level of the Galleria serves such provincial specialties as twice-cooked pork, shredded beef, and chicken with peanuts. L, D, Monday through Saturday. All major credit cards.

Inexpensive

Lucky Inn. 912 St. Emanuel (Chinatown); 228-1522. When it's the middle of the night and suddenly you've just got to have some chicken with snow peas or sweet and sour pork, this is the place. Lucky Inn has dependably good

Cantonese fare, and it has it until 10:00 P.M. on weekdays and 3:00 A.M. every weekend. You can also get a good cheap lunch cafeteria-style on weekdays. L, D, daily. AE, MC, V.

DELICATESSEN

Inexpensive

Butera's. 4621 Montrose (museum area); 523–0722 and 2946 S. Shepherd; 528–1500. With an ample dining room and tables out front under an awning, Butera's lines 'em up and packs 'em in every weekday at noon. A variety of sandwiches are made each day, but if you don't see what you want on the counter, just ask and they'll make it for you if the ingredients are on hand. The real calling card here is the wide selection of soups (occasionally overspiced) and salads (often underspiced). Try the green-bean salad with tomato and onion or the broccoli-cauliflower combo. Butera's has a wide selection of imported beers and wines at reasonable prices. B, daily (Montrose only); L, daily; D, Monday through Friday till eight. AE, MC, V.

New York Coffee Shop. 9720 Hillcroft (southwest); 723–8650. Expatriate New Yorkers flock to this pleasant coffee shop on weekend mornings to enjoy lox, eggs and onions, hot bagels with cream cheese, and other well-prepared deli-style favorites. It may be a long drive home, so pick up some bagels to go on the way out. B, L, daily. No credit cards.

Nielsen's. 4500 Richmond; 963–8005. You will keep coming back to this old-style deli for the tasty corned-beef sandwiches and creamy potato salad. If you're in a hurry, pick up one of the boxed lunches (a sandwich and a half, potato salad, brownies, and pickles). The cream cheese cake is made on the premises and is one of their claims to fame. Although they don't serve breakfast, they do open at 7 A.M. weekdays, 8 A.M. on Saturday, nice to know if you are putting together an all-day outing and need a lunch before you roll out of town. Open until 6 P.M. weekdays; 4 P.M. on Saturday. No credit cards.

FRENCH-CONTINENTAL

Deluxe to Super Deluxe

La Reserve. Four Riverway, in the Inn on the Park (Magic Circle); 871–8177. La Reserve has established its reputation as one of Houston's very best dining spots, particularly for *nouvelle cuisine*. This elegant establishment also offers one of the best deals in the city: *Le Grand Menu.* You get seven courses—a selection of the chef's specials of the day, including two appetizers, two entrées (in smaller-than-normal portions), a salad, a cheese, and dessert. The pheasant mousse and sweetbreads are grand, and try the Napoleon when the pastry wagon comes around. L, Monday through Friday; D, Monday through Saturday. All major credit cards.

Les Continents. 5150 Westheimer in the Intercontinental Hotel (Galleria); 961–9313. One of the least sung but best of the fine restaurants in town, this handsome room with its dark peach appointments and fine service is just the spot when only something *très* elegant will do. Will it be the fresh redfish poached in champagne? The Assiette des Pecheurs? The Supreme de Volaille Dauphinoise? From classics to nouvelle, Beluga caviar to the fresh pastries on the dessert trolley, the food is memorable. No regrets, even when you get the equally rarified check. Note that this tucked-away place often closes in summer; check on hours when you call for reservations. D, Monday through Saturday. All major credit cards.

Tony's. 1801 S. Post Oak (Magic Circle); 622–6778. Tony's has long had a reputation as the best restaurant in Houston. This is the place to dine if you hope to parley with the powerful, hobnob with the *haut monde*, blend with the big shots. Of course, it helps if you *are* a powerful big shot. The regular patrons get extremely attentive service, and it has on more than one occasion been at the expense of those outside their elite circle. That rather large caveat aside, a meal at Tony's can be exceptional. The secret to a superior meal? Dispense with the menu and ask your captain for his suggestions; several very good pasta dishes don't even appear on the menu. In fact, any unlisted special is likely to be just that—special. If it all becomes a bit overwhelming, remember: The grilled veal chop is stupendous, and the ambrosial raspberry soufflé would get a banker into heaven. L, Monday through Friday; D, Monday through Saturday. All major credit cards.

Deluxe

Maxim's. 3755 Richmond (Greenway Plaza); 877–8899. This eccentrically luxurious restaurant has been a local favorite for years, first downtown but more recently in the suburban climate of Greenway Plaza. The style of cooking is French Creole, and the most notable specialties are the crab dishes. Try the Charlie Bell salad made with lump crabmeat, or the delicious crabmeat with brown butter. L, Monday through Friday; D, Monday through Saturday. All major credit cards.

Moderate to Expensive

Brennan's. 3300 Smith (near downtown); 522–9711. No longer connected to the famous New Orleans French Quarter restaurant of the same name, Brennan's has a pleasing *vieux carre* atmosphere. Unfortunately, the food is not always up to expectations, but the simple dishes, such as steak Diane, are fairly dependable. On Saturdays, the jazz brunch adds to the New Orleansy flavor. L, Monday through Friday; D, daily; Brunch, Saturday and Sunday. All major credit cards.

Chez Eddy. 6560 Fannin, 4th fl. (Medical Center); 790–6474. Who says French food can't be good for you? In the heart of the Medical Center, this elegant restaurant features low sodium–low fat *nouvelle cuisine*. The fruit-and-yogurt dessert creations are better than anything this healthful has any right to be. L, Monday through Friday; D, Tuesday through Saturday. AE, MC, V.

Fuad's. 6100 Westheimer (southwest); 785–0130. This quasi-plush restaurant offers a number of Lebanese specialties along with the more conventional Continental fare. Veal à la Fuad—in a cream sauce with artichokes—is a notable feature of the menu. L, Monday through Friday; D, daily. All major credit cards.

L'Oeuf et le Lapin. 1172 Greens Parkway (Greenspoint area; call for directions); 875–6140. Known simply as the Egg and the Rabbit, this find of a place is the arena of French chef Philippe Carre and may be the best bargain for fine food in town. The two-course lunch is $6.96 and the four-course dinner, with your choice of 10–15 entrees, is $23.50. You may be so dazzled by the display of desserts you'll never get past the foyer. L, Monday through Friday; D, Monday through Saturday. All major credit cards.

GERMAN

Inexpensive

Bavarian Gardens. 3926 Feagan (Heights); 861–6300. This German beer hall serves up hearty renditions of wiener schnitzel, sauerbraten, and various sausages. Side dishes include formidable potato pancakes and zesty red cabbage. The resident oompah band does its most interesting work with cowbells and the large, mournful-sounding alp horns. During Oktoberfest (all month long) the outdoor *Biergarten* is packed with singing, swaying, dancing revelers. L, Monday through Friday; D, Monday through Saturday. No CB.

INDIAN

Inexpensive to Moderate

India's. 5704 Richmond (southwest); 266–0131. Houston is blessed with several fine Indian restaurants; this is one of the best. Tandoori chicken, boneless chicken *tikka,* and *nan* (a delicious flat bread) are among the treats that come from the clay tandoori oven. Other noteworthy specialties: *rogan josh* (lamb cooked in yogurt) and *sag paneer* (an amazing and wonderful sort of creamed spinach cooked with large chunks of a mild white cheese). L, D, daily. All major credit cards.

Taj Mahal. 8328 Gulf Freeway (southeast); 649–2818. Situated in an area not known for its stellar restaurants, the Taj Mahal is a great place to stop for dinner on your way out to Gilley's if you're interested in a real transcultural experience. The food is excellent, with a menu very similar to India's (the owner of India's and some of the kitchen staff are Taj Mahal alumni). The lunch buffet is a real bargain at $5.95. L, D, Tuesday through Sunday. All major credit cards.

ITALIAN

Moderate to Expensive

Carrabba's. 3115 Kirby (River Oaks/Rice University); 522–3131. There's often a wait at this popular place, so try to go off the standard dining hours. House specialties range from thin crust pizzas to fresh pasta and fish—ask for the day's features—and all sauces are made on-site with fresh ingredients. Pizza fans should start with the Margarita, made with fresh mozzarella, basil, and roma tomatoes; seafood lovers should pray that fresh red snapper or coho salmon is on the list of daily specials. Whatever you order, do include a salad topped with the house's parmesan dressing. You can watch the action in the open kitchen from a seat at the pizza bar. L, D, daily. All major credit cards.

Damian's. 3011 Smith (near downtown); 522–0439. This welcome addition to Houston's growing list of good Italian restaurants won't disappoint. For starters, sample the *Gnocchi Verde* (spinach dumplings with tomato and cream sauce) or the *Calamari Fritti* (fried squid). The *Taglierini BRV*—white, red and green pasta topped with cheese, mushrooms and zucchini—may be the perfect Italian dish. Popular entrees include *valigetta* (a suitcase of veal scallopini stuffed with fontana cheese and eggplant) and *involtini di pollo* (breast of chicken stuffed with Italian sausage and sauteed in wine). L, Monday through Friday; D, Monday through Saturday. All major cards.

Moderate

Nino's. 2817 W. Dallas (Montrose); 522–5120. A popular neighborhood restaurant, Nino's draws a large lunchtime crowd from nearby downtown. Standard Italian dishes are generally the best bet: Spaghetti with tomato sauce, meat sauce, or simply butter and garlic is dependably good; the hearty lasagna is tasty and filling. This is not food of great distinction, but most days it fills the bill very well, *grazie*. L, Monday through Friday; D, Monday through Saturday. All major credit cards.

Inexpensive

Allegro. 2407 Rice Blvd. (Rice University area); 526–4200. This Italian bakery in the Rice Village has become a real hot spot among the city's yuppies, and not without cause. The outdoor tables are just right for lingering over croissants and coffee. A menu of more substantial cold plates and salads offers sustenance for extended afternoons of people watching. The mint chicken salad in half a cantaloupe is a standout. B, L, D, daily; closes at 5 P.M. on Sunday.

The Olive Garden. 10830 Northwest Freeway; 682–1465. Call for other locations in Humble, Baybrook, and north Harris County. When a filling lunch ends up at $5 and dinner between $7 and $8, why go elsewhere for your lasagne, fettuccine Alfredo, or veal piccata? You can top off that meal with a slice of zuppa inglese, Italy's answer to the English trifle. Continuing the theme, these spacious restaurants have walls covered with Italian murals, ethnic electronic music, and a long list of Italian wines and beers. For Italian brew at its best, try Raffino. L, D, daily. All major credit cards.

MEXICAN

Inexpensive to Moderate

Armando's. 1811 S. Shepherd (Montrose); 521–9757. Though it's right next door to a Taco Bell, the food at this pleasant restaurant is light-years away from your basic burrito and beans and is about as close as Mexican cooking gets to being light and healthful. The menu has expanded to include steak and shrimp, but Armando's made its reputation with a variety of inventive chicken dishes. The chicken enchiladas are ever popular, and with good reason. The location is right across the street from the Comedy Workshop. L,D, daily. All major credit cards. It even has valet parking, surprising for a restaurant with prices so reasonable.

Merida. 2509 Navigation (north side), and other locations; 227–0260. Taking its name from the capital of Yucatán, Merida specializes in the cuisine of that southeastern region of Mexico. Order special No. 1, *cochinitas pibil,* a marinated pork roast, served with rice, black beans, onions, and soft flour tortillas. B, L, D, daily. All major credit cards.

Ninfa's. 2704 Navigation (north side), and other locations; 228–1175. Ninfa's is a treasured Houston institution. Every Houstonian over the age of four knows the stirring tale of how the widowed Mama Ninfa and her five children turned their struggling northside cantina (formerly a tortilla factory) into a prosperous statewide restaurant empire. They didn't do it by mouthing corny homilies about the American Dream, but by developing an extensive, creative menu. *Tacos al carbón* (aka *tacos a la Ninfa*), charbroiled beef wrapped in soft flour tortillas, are marvelous and made the place famous, but that's just the beginning. Some of the specialties here will forever disabuse epicurian snobs of the faulty notion that Mexican food is just a greasy, lowborn novelty. *Pechugas de pollo,* savory, marinated chicken breasts, are light but very satisfying. Tender chunks of deep-fried pork, called *carnitas,* served with sour cream and an explosive green chile sauce, are equally hard to pass up. Stay away from the Tex-Mex items, crispy tacos and such—they're fine, but you can get that sort of thing anywhere—and stick with Mama's special dishes, some of which aren't even on the regular menu. Ask your waiter about *alambre abrigado,* a sort of shish kebob of beef, ham, onions, peppers, and tomatoes chopped and rolled into flour tortillas; or *queso al suizo de pechuga,* tortillas stuffed with chicken and melted Swiss cheese. If you'd care to sample the *chilpanzingas,* ham and cheese turn-overs with a fiery afterburn, give the kitchen a day's advance notice so they can prepare the special corn-meal mixture that's needed. But one of the best things here is free and arrives on your table as soon as you sit down—fresh, hot tortilla chips served with little pitchers of red and green sauces. The green sauce is a creamy miracle, the possible ingredients of which offer a subject for continuing debate. Ninfa's no longer has the cachet of the out-of-the-way eatery known only to the cognoscenti, but it's impossible to keep food this good a secret. L, D, daily. All major credit cards.

Pappasito's. 6445 Richmond (Southwest); 784–5253, and 15280 North Free-way (North); 821–4505. Judging by the eternal crowds, these are just about the most popular Mexican restaurants in town. Justifiably so. The portions are huge, the menu varied, and there's a definite talent in the kitchen. If you can bypass the enchilada/taco choices, try the mesquite-grilled shrimp or the succulent *fajitas.* L,D, daily. AE, MC, V.

Primo's. 519 Rosalie at Smith (near downtown); 528–9158. Also 77 Harvard at Washington (Heights); 862–0766. Tex-Mex items abound on the menu, but the reason to eat at Primo's is the best Mexican-style steak in town. Called *fajitas,* this marinated skirt steak is thick, juicy, and comparatively tender. (This is never a particularly tender cut of meat, and in many restaurants it is served dry and rather tough.) The *carne guisada,* stewed chunks of beef in a spicy tomato sauce, is also quite good. L, D, daily. AE, MC, V.

Spanish Village. 4720 Almeda (near the Medical Center); 523–1727. This restaurant is in a somewhat marginal neighborhood but continues to draw large and festive crowds for both lunch and dinner. The food is greasy but quite tasty and filling. The cheese-and-onion enchiladas are classics. L, D, Tuesday through Saturday. AE, MC, V.

Tila's Cantina. 616 Westheimer (Montrose); 520–6315. The combination of fresh ingredients and inventive recipes gives Tila's real flair. The Mexican/New American Cuisine is served up in an art deco-ish building with a great view of the notorious Westheimer strip. L, Tuesday through Sunday; D, daily. AE, MC, V.

Inexpensive

Cortes Meat Market and Delicatessen. 2404 W. Alabama (Kirby); 522–7771. This tiny lunch counter–dining room between trendy Montrose and exclusive River Oaks serves up generous plates of sturdy Mexican food, including beef tips with rice and beans, Tampico crepes with lobster sauce and guacamole, and beef or bean tacos. This is also a popular spot on weekend mornings for Mexican breakfasts. B, L, Tuesday through Sunday; D, Tuesday through Friday. No credit cards.

MOROCCAN

Moderate to Expensive

Casablanca. 14025 Memorial (Memorial); 531–9060. This well-decorated restaurant surely seems authentic: You sit on the floor and eat with your fingers. (Yes, there is a belly dancer.) Main-course selections include quail, shrimp, veal, lamb *cous-cous,* and a commendable Cornish hen served with preserved lemon or a honey-and-garlic sauce. All meals have five courses and include soup, marinated vegetables, and *b'stilla,* a delicious, flaky pastry filled with chicken and nuts and dusted with confectioner's sugar. D, Tuesday through Sunday. AE, MC, V.

SEAFOOD

Moderate to Expensive

Bayou City Oyster Company. 2171 Richmond; 523–6640. Fresh oysters on the half-shell are just the start of a fine meal here. Or maybe you would prefer an unusual version of oysters Rockefeller loaded with bacon but little spinach. There are grilled seafood dishes as well. L, D, daily. All credit cards accepted.

Don's. 3009 S. Post Oak (Magic Circle); 629–5380. The large numbers of people packed into the oyster bar and waiting for a table at Don's should tip you off: This restaurant serves some of the best seafood in town. The Louisiana-style specialties include seafood gumbo, crawfish étouffée, fried catfish, and stuffed shrimp. For such a noisy, crowded place, Don's is awfully comfortable, thanks largely to the very friendly service. L, D, daily. All major credit cards.

Magnolia Bar and Grill. 6000 Richmond (southwest); 781–6207. Enjoy a dozen fresh oysters shucked to order while you make up your mind. It's not easy choosing among the Cajun seafood dishes. Crawfish are available in season (December through June), but don't forget the frog legs, shrimp and soft-shelled crab. L, D, daily. All major cards.

Moderate

The Anchorage. 2504 North Loop West; 688–4411. Often overlooked as new "formula" restaurants come on the scene, the Anchorage can be relied on for outstanding swordfish, abalone, and shrimp, as well as such classics as red snapper Charlie Brown. All are fresh, tasty, and affordable. B, L, D, daily. All major credit cards.

Atchaflaya River Cafe. 8816 Westheimer at Fondren; (975–7873). First, so you'll sound like a southerner, it's pronounced "chafa-lie-a." Second, this is one of the best places in town for blackened redfish, andouille sausage, and other Cajun necessities of life. The sound system decibels are exceeded only by the size of the crowd, but the food is good and the fun level high. L,D, daily. AE, MC, V.

The Back Bay. 1200 McKinney (The Park at Houston Center); 739–7484. A New Wave seafood restaurants, courtesy of the blue neon wave logo on the wall. Good place to fill up on blackened redfish, lobster fajitas, and other trendy pescado. Check to see if they have any fresh oysters from South Padre, an unsung Lone Star treat. Very casual and a favorite meeting spot for downtown business types. L, D, weekdays, until 6 P.M. on Saturday. All major credit cards.

Captain Benny's Half Shell. 7409 S. Main (between the Medical Center and the Astrodome), and other locations; 795–9051. There are no tables in this tiny boat-shaped building, so elbow your way up to the bar and holler out your order for a dozen of the best oysters in Houston, fresh from Matagorda Bay. And if you've never tried catfish, please don't miss this chance. You'll wonder how anything with whiskers could taste so good. L, D, Monday through Saturday. No credit cards.

Pappas Seafood. 694 Southwest Freeway (call for other locations); 784–4729. The fish always is fresh here, and the portions are almost enough to feed two. Go ahead—order one plate and two forks; this eatery is used to it. The menu is large and ranges from oysters through all manner of seafood to roast beef, and the salads are meals in themselves. L,D, daily. AE, MC, V.

Inexpensive

Glatzmaier's Seafood Market. 809 Congress (on Market Square downtown); 223–3331. This noisy, cafeteria-style fish house is a fun lunch spot, especially when Big Joe Danza is over in the corner pounding on the piano. When things quiet down, the atmosphere in this antique room with its churning ceiling fans is remindful of a lazy afternoon in some French Quarter oyster bar. Generous plates of fried fish with a crispy corn-meal batter draw long lines every weekday. The broccoli with cheese and "Mama's potatoes" may just be the best steam-table vegetables ever. A new second location at 4704 Montrose in the museum area also is open for dinner daily. L, Monday through Friday. No credit cards.

STEAK

Deluxe

Brenner's. 10911 Katy Freeway (northwest); 465–2901. This homey little steakhouse on the I–10 East access road (take the Wilcrest exit about a dozen miles west of downtown and make a U-turn back toward the east) is pretty special. It serves the best steaks in Houston, and perhaps the world (partisans of Ruth's Chris Steakhouse will probably give you an argument). But the crispy-chewy German-fried potatoes with onions or the tart homemade Roquefort dressing alone would be reason enough to bestow world-class honors on Mrs. Brenner's kitchen. Service is very friendly. The woodsy dining room overlooks a peculiarly charming backyard diorama, which blocks out the view of the freeway. This may be the perfect Houston restaurant. L, Tuesday through Friday, and Sunday; D, Tuesday through Sunday. All major credit cards.

The Palm. 6100 Westheimer (southwest); 977–2544. This Houston version of the famous New York restaurant naturally serves up incredible steaks. The lobsters are large enough to be frightening, especially since you pay by the pound. L, Monday through Friday; D, daily. All major credit cards.

Ruth's Chris Steakhouse. 6213 Richmond (southwest); 789–2333. This New Orleans–style steakhouse is quite popular with people in the oil business, as evidenced by all the oil-company logos that adorn the place. Most steaks (as well as the side dishes) are large enough to feed two people. Feel free to divide an order or ask for a doggie bag. L, Sunday through Friday; D, Monday through Saturday. All major credit cards.

Moderate

The Hofbrau. 1803 Shepherd (Heights); 869–7074. A local incarnation of an Austin institution, this funky steakhouse is something of a shrine for University of Texas graduates, apparently fulfilling some spiritual need between pilgrimages to the real thing. The steaks, cooked in lemon butter, may not be all that tender, but they are quite flavorful. And besides, this is a lot of fun. L, Monday through Friday; D, daily. AE, MC, V.

Steak and Ale. 5000 Richmond (Magic Circle), and other locations; 965–0351. A chain operation with outlets all over town, Steak and Ale serves decent steaks, prime rib, and lobster, but we mention it primarily because it's convenient. There was a time when they didn't serve ale, but that little problem of faulty advertising has been corrected since the Molson brewing company of Canada began distributing their products in the Lone Star State. L, Monday through Friday; D, daily. All major credit cards.

Inexpensive

Texas Tumbleweed. 2044 East T.C. Jester (call for other locations); 861–0180. Decent steaks cooked over mesquite and live country and western music are the primary draws at this chain establishment. L, Monday through Fridays; D, Monday through Saturday. AE, DC, MC, V.

THAI

Inexpensive to Moderate

Morningside Thai. 6710 Morningside; 669–8223. How does curried beef in coconut sauce or spicy sate sound? This is a good spot for a first venture into Thai cuisine. L, Sunday through Friday; L, D, daily. All major credit cards.

Thai Orchid. 8282 Bellaire; 981–7006. Another good choice in the southwestern part of town. Start off with the crab delight as an appetizer and then shift to the delightfully light spring rolls. The stir-fried chicken or beef makes a good entree. Best of all, the spicy sauces come on the side, so you can fix all to your own taste. L, daily; D, Tuesday through Sunday. All major credit cards.

Thai Pepper. 2049 W. Alabama (Montrose); 520–8225. This attractive place is developing a strong repeat clientele. Deep-fried cheese rolls served with a sweet sauce for dipping are an unusual appetizer. The lime beef, an incendiary salad of marinated beef, lettuce, tomatoes, onions, and peppers tossed in a spicy sauce is guaranteed to wake up your taste buds. Cool off with some coconut ice cream for dessert. L, Monday through Friday; D, daily. AE, MC, V.

VIETNAMESE

Inexpensive

Mai Que. 2404 W. Holcombe (near the Medical Center); 663–6544. Mai Que (pronounced "My Way") has dozens of Vietnamese specialties from which to choose on its menu. The soft pan-fried egg noodle dishes with your choice of beef, chicken, or shrimp are particularly good. The Vietnamese Muzak, however, is definitely an acquired taste. L, D, daily. All major credit cards.

Viet Nam Kitchen. 2929C Milam (near downtown); 520–7106. This pleasant restaurant on the southern edge of downtown offers a varied and extensive Vietnamese menu. Some very good dishes are quite inexpensive, such as the *bun thit nuong* (charcoal broiled pork with vermicelli) and the *bun bo xao* (vermicelli with beef). Summer rolls (called *goi cuon*), shrimp, pork, vegetables, and vermicelli rolled in rice paper, make a nice appetizer for two. By all means have the iced French coffee for dessert. L, D, daily. MC, V, AE, DC.

Vietnam Restaurant. 3215 Main (near downtown); 526–0917. Imperial rolls and spring rolls, served with a cool plate of sliced cucumber, lettuce, mint, and other greens are just right for a light snack or as an appetizer. The crab dishes are among the proprietor's recommended specialties. L, D, daily. AE, MC, V.

 NIGHTLIFE. Houston's nightly entertainment choices are many and diverse. Our best-known night spot is certainly Gilley's, the honkytonk immortalized by the movie *Urban Cowboy*. Gilley's and the other country-and-western joints listed here provide entertainment and atmosphere that don't exist in many parts of the country; they're a part of our regional identity. But if you're one of those people who for some curious reason hates country music, relax—there are clubs aplenty that feature rock 'n' roll, jazz, disco, even comedy if you'd rather laugh than listen. Or if you're simply in search of a quiet drink and perhaps a little conversation, you'll find that as well. Bars and nightclubs generally stay open until 2:00 A.M., but a surprising number close at midnight; call and check if you plan to be out late. Many take credit cards, but again, call first if you want to avoid depleting your cash reserves. And remember: It may be a long drive back to your hotel, and it's a tough town in which to catch a cab should you find yourself a victim of intemperance. So watch your intake—you want to call the boss in the morning to tell him that he just acquired a new subsidiary, not that he needs to wire bail money.

COUNTRY-AND-WESTERN DANCE HALLS

Al Marks Melody Ballroom. 3027 Crossview (southwest, between Richmond and Westheimer); 785–5301. Tuesday nights draw a dressed-up singles crowd for some ballroom dancing to DJ music. Friday nights, live bands bring back the Big Band era of the '40s, and on Sundays it's country and western, again with a DJ. There's a 2200-sq.-ft. dance floor, plus a cash bar, free parking, and heavy security in the parking lot.

Bill's Country Palace. 835 W. 34th (North Heights); 862–5990. A long-time favorite for all kinds of dancing, this place has a dance floor the size of a basketball court and attracts a well-mannered crowd. Open only once a month in winter and on Friday and Sunday evenings in the spring and fall, and it really cranks up for C&W on Wednesday, Friday, and Sunday evenings in the summer.

Dance Town USA. 7214 Airline Drive (north side); 697–2083. Open Wednesdays and Saturdays, Dance Town sells beer, wine, and setups; BYOB if you want something stronger. Very good local recording artists headline here, including country and western groups like Westwood, Telstars, and the Snider Brothers.

Eddie's Country Ballroom. FM 1128 in Manvel (6 miles west of Pearland); 489–8181. This BYOB place swings with live C&W weekends. Call for directions and to learn who is playing when you're ready to kick up your heels south of town.

Gilley's Club. 4500 Spencer Highway, Pasadena; *Urban Cowboy* may have cast the national spotlight on this sprawling honkytonk (it once billed itself as the world's largest, an honor now claimed by Billy Bob's in Fort Worth), but Gilley's was a legend in these parts long before John Travolta learned to two-step. Aside from the busloads of tourists, things haven't changed that much. The atmosphere is remindful of a carnival or county fair; more people are lookin' for love than are lookin' for a fight, and some folks even bring the kids. You can still ride the mechanical bull, be a real man at the punching-bag machine, and play pool, pinball, and video games. Or you can dance to excellent music provided by some of the biggest names in country music. As large as Gilley's is (about five acres), it gets crowded to the point of claustrophobia when popular fellas like Jerry Jeff Walker or Willie Nelson are in town. The latest addition to the Gilley's empire is a rodeo arena right next door to the club. The cover charge varies, depending on who's on stage.

Sons of Hermann Skyline Ballroom. 147 Heights Blvd. (Heights, north of I–10); 862–0018. There's always live music here on Saturday nights year-round and on the third Wednesday of the month. If you are pooped, come for bingo on Fridays. Mostly local Houston bands play ballroom tunes; the fourth Saturday of the month features C&W with the Nashville Express. Beer, wine, soft drinks, and setups are available. If you want something stronger, you are welcome to BYOB.

POP/ROCK/FOLK

The Ale House. 2425 W. Alabama (Montrose); 521–2333. This extremely casual music club offers everything from New Wave to funk, jazz fusion to rockabilly.

Anderson Fair. 2007 Grant at Welch (Montrose); 528–8576. Time stopped in 1967 at this Montrose-area institution. This home for aging hippies provides a stage for local folkies and touring legends such as Dave Van Ronk and Houston's own Townes Van Zandt.

Blythe Spirits. 614 W. Gray; 529–7496. What passes for punk in Houston is here, enjoying new-wave rock at megadecibels. Young scene.

Bourbon Street. 2030 Bingle (west side at Hammerly); 984–1931. Popular with the 25–45 set, this casual place features rock as well as rhythm and blues. Shake Russell often headlines here, along with Miss Molly and the Passions, one of the current rages of Houston. Monday night's Performer Spotlight showcases fresh local talent.

Caribana. 8220 W. Bellfort. Houston's first reggae club brings those Jamaican rhythms to the southwest side of town.

Chelsea's 804 Club. 804 Chelsea Place (Montrose); 527–8104. A variety of music is offered here, ranging from New Orleans jazz piano to blues guitar, but the emphasis is on rhythm and blues and rock. Sunday nights are Songwriter's Showcase. Drop in, you may be one of the first to hear a new hit.

Fitzgerald's. 2706 White Oak at Studewood (Heights); 862–7580. Originally a Polish meeting hall, Fitzgerald's is host to some of the best up-tempo rock and blues on the Gulf coast and regularly features the New Orleans sounds of the Neville Brothers, the Nuevo Wavo music of Joe King Carasco, and such dissimilar types as fiddler Vassar Clements and New Wave instrumentalists the Raybeats. The stage acts perform upstairs. Downstairs is a comfortably time-worn neighborhood bar.

The Metropole. 1997 Waugh Drive (Montrose); 524–9840. The Metropole started out as a private club, but that idea didn't go over too well in egalitarian Houston. Then it featured jazz exclusively. Now the emphasis is on the top of pop Wednesday through Sunday. Cover on the weekends.

Rockfeller's. 3620 Washington (Heights); 861–9365. Housed in a grand old bank building, this can be the best music room in town if you choose your seat properly. Pay the few extra dollars to reserve a table downstairs in the center of the room. Some seats off to the side have an obstructed view; the sound is unpredictable in the balcony. This is *the* club for touring musicians. The diverse lineup runs from jazz to bluegrass and has in the past featured Stephane Grapelli, Buddy Rich, Flora Purim, the Pointer Sisters, David Grisman, Ricky Skaggs, Doc Watson, Jose Feliciano, Harry James, Herbie Mann, Dizzy Gillespie, Roy Orbison, Doc Severinson, Riders in the Sky, Delbert McClinton, and scores of others. The crowd here can be inattentive and overtalkative, which is annoying when you've paid up to $15 cover. There is a full bar.

Wunche Brothers Cafe and Saloon. 103 Midway, Spring (north of Houston via I–45); 353–2825. This old frame building is a historic landmark, and the cafe has been famous for its hamburgers for generations. The music ranges from rhythm and blues to Shake Russell rock, folk songs, and C&W. There's a surprisingly strong family trade here, and the outside upstairs deck is a good place to be with a cold beer on a warm summer evening. Lot's of Texas redneck color here.

JAZZ

Blue Moon. 1010 Banks (Montrose); 523–3773. Live jazz and one of the best munchie menus in town. Good spot for after theater drinks. Dress up some; this place draws a classy crowd.

Cody's. 3400 Montrose (Montrose); 522–9747. About 2½ mi. from downtown, this glassed-in room and roof terrace atop a 10-story building offers the best view in town of Houston's changing skyline. It's also been home at one time or another for two of Houston's best young jazzmen: pianist Paul English and saxophonist Kirk Whalum. No cover; two-drink minimum. A fairly casual dress code (no sneakers, jeans, or T-shirts) is rather strictly enforced.

DISCO/DANCING

Westin Galleria Hotel, 5060 W. Alabama (Galleria II); 960–8100. On the 24th floor of the Westin Galleria Hotel, this rooftop hot spot caters to a very well-dressed bunch of young professionals. Danceable top 40s tunes predominate here, and the cover charge varies $1–3, depending on the day of the week.

The Copa. 2631 Richmond at Kirby (near Greenway Plaza); 528–2250. This shopping-center club has a mixed clientele of gay and straight dancers. Disco and rock 'n' roll blare from a very expensive sound system.

Fast and Cool Club. 6135 Kirby (Rice University); 528–3456. Known to the post-college, young professional set as a good place for serious, energetic dancing, this popular club features the best music of the 60s, 70s, and 80s, complete with brightly painted dancers in cages around the dance floor.

Hippo. 6400 Richmond (Southwest); 789–7707. An explosive light show strobes and throbs its way through the evening and dancing goes on until 4 A.M., creating one of the latest action scenes in town. The free 5–8 P.M. weekday buffet ranges from Mexican to seafood, and there's no cover until 9 P.M. Visually hard to miss, this high-tech place has a clean and casual dress code; plays progressive top-40 tunes and classic rock during happy hour; and rocks with the latest and hottest new music through the night.

Numbers. 300 Westheimer (Montrose); 526–6551. This large disco on the Westheimer strip is something of an old established landmark in the heart of Houston's gay community. New wave music is the theme here.

HOTEL AND PIANO BARS

The Bagatelle. Doubletree Hotel, 400 Dallas (downtown); 759–0202. Partitioned off from the rest of the lobby with attractive carved limestone panels, this swanky little corner features a pianist on Saturday evenings.

Bistro Vino. 819 W. Alabama at Roseland; 526–5500. Windows of this old stucco home surround you as soft piano music soothes you in the setting of a French and Italian bistro and bar. An easygoing but elegant setting is topped with good food, served Monday through Friday.

The Black Swan. Inn on the Park, 4 Riverway (Magic Circle); 871–8181. This is just one spot in which to enjoy a drink in the elegant Inn on the Park, tucked away in its own quiet corner of one of the city's most rapidly developing areas. One may also imbibe at the Palm Court or the adjacent lobby piano bar.

Brittany Bar. Lincoln Hotel, 2001 S. Post Oak (Magic Circle); 961–9300. Most of the public spaces in this I. M. Pei–designed hotel have a feeling of monastic simplicity, but this wood-paneled bar tucked off an interior court has an almost pub-like atmosphere.

City Lights. Stouffer's Hotel, 6 Greenway Plaza East; 629–1200. Who says it's lonely at the top? Join the gang at this watering hole on the roof of Stouffer's. Unfortunately, the view of southwest Houston is blocked in some directions by taller buildings.

La Colombe d'Or. 3410 Montrose (Montrose); 524–7999. This "European"-style hotel and restaurant occupies the old Fondren mansion. The Fondrens were one of the founding families of the Humble (now Exxon) Oil fortune. The atmosphere and the prices may be far from humble in both the wine bar and the Cognac lounge, but the selection of wines and Cognacs is indeed extensive.

Hunt Room. Warwick Hotel, 5701 S. Main (museum area); 526–1991. The bar of Houston's most traditional hotel; drinks are also served by the piano in the lobby.

The Irish Pub–Kenneally's. 2111 S. Shepherd; 630–0486. It is what its name says it is: a fine bar with dark wood, and brogue floats through the air. The live music is, of course, Irish. Open daily.

Pete's Pub. Hotel Intercontinental, 5150 Westheimer; 961–1500. Plush and soothing, this darkly paneled retreat has a 1920s speakeasy theme. Expect soft live music during happy hour from 4 to 9 P.M.

Pierre's. Adams Mark Hotel, 2900 Briarpark at Westheimer (southwest); 978–7400. You'll find this hotel piano bar on the western edge of town featuring jazz sometimes, depending on who's playing.

The Roof. Westin Oaks Hotel, 5011 Westheimer (Galleria); 623–4300. On the 21st floor of the Westin Oaks Hotel, this is just the spot to hide out when the rigors of shopping become too much. If you're lucky, you might catch Kirk Whalum, Houston's hot young saxophone genius.

Spindletop. Hyatt Regency, 1200 Louisiana (downtown); 654–1234. What booming Sun Belt city could live without a John Portman–designed hotel with a revolving bar on top? The downtown construction boom has eliminated the panoramic views in many directions, so drinkers now must content themselves with views of towering workaholics in the office buildings that surround the hotel.

Terrace Cafe. Four Seasons Hotel, 1300 Lamar (downtown); 650–1300. This handsome room trimmed in polished brass and etched glass serves a good drink and has live entertainment.

COMEDY CLUBS

Comedy Showcase. 12260 Gulf Freeway (southeast, near Almeda Mall); 947–0823. Local and regional standup comics perform every night but Monday.

Comedy Workshop & Comix Annex. 2105 San Felipe at Shepherd (Montrose); 524–7333. The first and best of Houston's comedy clubs features original musical revues in the cabaret. Next door at the Annex standup comics do their stuff. Weekends are reserved for the pros. Earlier in the week, the old hands try out new material and fledgling funnymen find out that sometimes comedy is no laughing matter.

Laff Stop. 1952A W. Gray (River Oaks); 524–2333. This well-appointed club in the River Oaks Shopping Center hosts touring professional comics—not the big names, but the young Turks who are just breaking on to the talk shows. Magicians are also featured on occasion.

Magic Island. 2215 Southwest Freeway (U.S. 59); 526–2442. Originally a private club, this fun place now is open to the public with gourmet dinners, Las Vegas–style magic and comedy shows, fortune tellers, astrologists, palm readers —the works. Check out the Monday through Thursday $25 special.

Radio Music Theatre. 1840 Westheimer; 522–7722. Return with us to the fun of an old-time radio show with musical comedy reviews Thursday through Saturday night.

Spellbinder's Comedy Club. 10001 Westheimer; 266–2525. The Wednesday through Sunday shows feature big name pros, three nightly, at this far-west club.

 BARS. An appropriate place to start a Houston bar tour is **downtown** Market Square, *La Carafe,* 813 Congress (229–9399), occupies the oldest commercial building in town. It's been a stagecoach stop, an Indian trading post, and a brothel, though today your pleasures are limited to beer, wine, and an excellent jukebox with selections from most everyone from Piaf to Blondie. Across the square is *Warren's Inn,* at 316 Milam (226–9362). Warren's, too, has an entertaining, if somewhat eccentric, jukebox selection (Ed Ames! Cheryl Ladd!), but is best known for a curious affliction: a plague of bats. Really. But that was several years ago; the strangest creatures to hang out there recently have been the Urban Animals, a fierce-looking but fairly benign roller-skating gang. Among the more traditional bars in the downtown area are *Fat Ernie's,*

behind the Hyatt Regency at 500 Dallas (658–1802), and the bar at *Brennan's,* 3300 Smith (522–9711), which has a quiet New Orleansy courtyard and serves a well-prepared sazerac cocktail or milk punch.

A few miles to the northeast of downtown, across the bayou, are two notorious ship-channel bars. The *Athens Bar and Grill,* 8037 Clinton (675–1644), dispenses large volumes of retsina and good Greek food to homesick Greek sailors and the rest of a motley crew that enjoys belly dancing and jovial rowdiness. Right around the corner, at 2327 McCarty, is *Harbor Lights* (673–9221), a beacon for thirsty sailors and certifiable eccentrics since 1931. (If the lady dancing next to you has a tattoo, try not to gawk.) The decor includes a map showing Nevada whorehouses. This isn't the sort of neighborhood where you're likely to need such a map, but be careful unless you're really a tough customer.

MONTROSE

To the west of downtown, south of the bayou, is the Montrose neighborhood, which is often compared to New York's Greenwich Village. (The resemblance is more philosophical than physical.) Home of hipsters, gays, young professionals, blacks, chicanos, and rednecks, Montrose is the most diverse and tolerant of the city's neighborhoods. In the heart of this cultural melting pot is *Grif's Shillelagh Inn,* 3416 Roseland (528–9912). More than just another Irish bar, Grif's is the unofficial headquarters of Houston's most avid sports fans. After big games, you'd almost think you were in the locker room. Another Montrose-area taproom that's more than just another Irish bar is *Birraporetti's,* 1997 W. Gray (529–9191), in the River Oaks Shopping Center. It's an Irish bar that happens to be in the middle of an Italian restaurant. You try to figure it. Around the corner, behind the River Oaks Theater, is an unmarked door beneath a fire escape at 2006 Peden. This is *Marfreless* (528–0083), a lovers' hideaway full of cozy couches in secluded nooks. Taped classical music adds to the romance. Across W. Gray, still in the River Oaks Center, is the *Wine Press,* 1962 W. Gray (528–6030), where you can enjoy wine by the bottle or by the glass, a wide selection of beers, and any brand of Scotch you can name. Over on the south side of the neighborhood, *Zimm's,* a wine bar at 4319 Montrose (529–4600), offers more than 200 different wines and daily wine specials by the glass for those who wish to sample the grape in moderation. This, along with a few neighboring establishments, is the closest thing in Houston to a sidewalk café.

ICE HOUSES

Houston does have a traditional sort of drinking establishment not unlike the sidewalk café, but most of them have been around longer than the sidewalks. Ice houses are the humble forerunners of the convenience store (7-11 started out as an ice house) and date from the days when people bought big chunks of block ice to cool the icebox. On hot days the thoughtful proprietors of these establishments started a tradition by keeping a few bottles of beer on ice for thirsty customers. Refrigerators ruined the market for block ice, but there's still no better way to cool a brew, as any knowledgeable Texan will gladly tell you. You'll recognize an ice house by the open garage doors across the front that let in the breeze, usually a few picnic tables scattered around the yard, and perhaps a horseshoe game in progress out under the oaks. Though sober-minded prigs may look upon this noble institution and see only an all-day picnic for alcoholics, right-thinking people have widely hailed the ice house as the poor man's country club. One of newest is *Mike and Tony's* (827–7520), in the Spring Branch area west of downtown at 1500 Bingle, but you'll find others in any of the city's older neighborhoods. Near Rice University are the *Poor Man's Country Club,* 2407 University (528–8396) and *Munchies,* 2349 Bissonnet (528–3545). The latter has a cosmopolitan twist: imported beer and live chamber music. Only in Houston.

THE GALLERIA AREA

If you'd prefer a more up-to-date spot to pursue your pleasures, head west to the Galleria area, where you'll find the greatest concentration of singles bars in the city. Behind the Galleria, in the 5000 block of Richmond, is the Windsor Plaza Shopping Center. At one end, you'll find *Friday's,* 5010 Richmond (627–3430), offering scores upon scores of specialty drinks at the raised bar in the center of the restaurant ("The better to see you, my dear"). At the far end of this strip center is *Cooter's,* 5164 Richmond (961–7494), which entertains a fun-loving crowd with ladies' nights on Mondays and Wednesdays. Happy hour runs all the way from 3:00 to 9:00 P.M. during the week. Other area hot spots include the bar at *On The Border,* a Tex-Mex restaurant, 4608 Westheimer (961–4494); the *Ocean Club,* 1885 St. James (963–9314), a multi-level see-and-be-seen place for the post-college set; and the *R & R USA,* 5351 W. Alabama (840–9720), popular with the 25–40 crowd early on in the evening, the young chic later. Both of the latter serve outstanding free gourmet buffets, usually during weekday happy hours. Call for current offerings, and you'll be able to skip dinner. Both pulse with progressive contemporary to high energy disco sounds. A bit farther afield, you'll find *Todd's,* 7901 SW Freeway (777–2527), one of Houston's oldest singles bars which attracts a young crowd with a DJ and top-40 format; and *Hippo,* 6400 Richmond (789–7707), is immediately recognizable with its black and pink paint job, topped off with an orange and pink awning. (The dress code is casual, but leave your faded jeans—"designer jeans preferred"—at home, along with your sandals, tennis shoes and shorts.) For gentlemen with no interest in meaningful relationships there's Houston's most notorious strip joint, *Caligula XXI,* 2618 Winrock (974–3867). The ladies at Caligula are skilled practitioners of a regional specialty known as couch dancing. How to describe couch dancing? Well . . . it's not for the germ conscious. *Rick's Restaurant and Bar,* 3113 Bering Drive (785–0444), is considered one of the classiest burlesque clubs in town.

Southwest Houston probably has more bars per square mile than any other part of the city; naturally, not all of them are geared toward real or imagined couplings (though you never know where the magic will strike). *Houlihan's Old*

Place, 1800 S. Post Oak (621–1740), is conveniently next door to one of Houston's first-run moviehouses and offers free hors d'oeuvres during happy hour, including an oyster bar on some days. Another popular happy-hour spot is a country-and-western disco called *San Antone Rose,* 1641 S. Voss at San Felipe (977–7116). Instead of a mirror ball above the dance floor, look for a lighted wagon wheel. The records, of course, are more likely to be by Waylon and Willie than by Donna Summer. But if you've had it with bars that follow one trend or another, drop in to the *Dark Horse Tavern,* 5706 Richmond (781–0322), a resolutely untrendy spot with more of a neighborhood feel than most of the bars in this part of town. A couple of blocks up the road you'll find the *Richmond Arms,* 5921 Richmond (977–8635), an English-style pub where Houston's expatriate Brits gather to throw a few darts. If you'd like to wind up the evening with even more of an "international" flair, venture on out to the 10000 block of Westheimer, where you'll discover the Carillon West Shopping Center, a Houston developer's vision of a quaint European village (complete with bell tower). Here you'll find *Sherlock's Baker Street Pub,* 10001 Westheimer (977–1857), and *The Great Caruso,* 10001 Westheimer (780–4900), where you can drink and dine while a troupe entertains with Broadway show tunes and light opera. Beer lovers should sample the more than 230 brands available at *T.V. Rovers,* just north of Westheimer on Highway 6 in far west Houston (496–0623). This is a good place also for a game of darts.

Still undecided? You can always pick up a six-pack and drive around. At the *Beverage Barn,* 9204 Richmond, between Fondren and Gessner (783–2407), you can drive the car right through the store and grab whatever you need, from milk to beer to a pint of your favorite. Cheers.

GALVESTON

by
FRANCES KAY HARRIS

Frances Kay Harris, a member of the Society of American Travel Writers, has been Travel Editor of the Galveston Daily News *for more than two decades and does a daily forty-five-minute radio show that deals largely with travel. A longtime resident of Galveston, she is a graduate of the University of Texas and has been an actress on Broadway.*

Galveston Island has been a family resort as far back as the days when the Karankawa indians used to pile the wife and kiddies into their canoes and paddle the two miles from the mainland to hunt deer and fowl and to fish on the beach. At least, this is what they were doing in 1528, when the Spaniards first discovered the island.

As time passed, despite the overabundance of snakes, the rumors that the Karankawas were fond of human flesh, and the fact that the island lay in the path of virulent storms, it still attracted many folks from many flags.

In 1817 Jean Laffite established a full camp in Galveston, using it as a base during his privateering days. Privateering differs from pirating in that the privateer is authorized by his government to seize enemy ships, whereas a pirate is in business for himself and takes his loot indiscriminately. Laffite is reputed to have been a true patriot and not the villain some histories have made him out to be. It is still believed by some local optimists that he might have left a bit of his treasure buried under Galveston sands. A plaque marks the place where his house is believed to have been.

Although the island lived under only five flags (the French didn't make any effort to occupy the area), Galveston was active in shucking the rule of the Spanish, then of Mexico, and it assisted in the Texas War of Independence. Once the Republic of Texas was established in 1836, the city of Galveston applied for a charter.

In 1839 Michael B. Menard drew up plans for a city. The design makes it very easy to get around in Galveston to this day. All the streets running east and west are labeled alphabetically (Avenues B, C, etc.), and those going the mile and a half between the Gulf of Mexico to the south and Galveston Bay in the north are numbered.

A great deal of Galveston now dates from no earlier than the 1900 storm. In September of that year an unheralded hurricane and giant tidal waves almost demolished this thirty-two-mile-long sandbar. When the disaster was over, more than six thousand people were dead, the port was destroyed, and most of the island's buildings were rubble.

Nevertheless, the islanders rebuilt Galveston. A seventeen-foot concrete seawall was constructed to protect the city from the wave action of the Gulf. Behind this bulwark, with sand dredged from surrounding channels and bayous, the entire town was raised, from seventeen feet at the south-end side to about six feet near the bay. This included streets, pipes, and houses. It was a mammoth undertaking but proved as effective as hoped when in 1915 an even more powerful storm swept over Galveston and relatively few (275) lives were lost.

The first seawall was less than four miles long. Over the years it has been lengthened, until today it extends for more than ten miles from the east end of the island. It is the longest continuous sidewalk in the world.

Galveston has several names. It is called Treasure Island, thanks to Jean Laffite, and the Oleander City because every street and most yards have many bushes of the single-, double-, and triple-petaled blossoms, ranging in colors from an almost blue-white, through yellows, through a great variety of pinks, to deep reds. During April and May the entire city is ablaze with these brilliant blooms. Yet another name for Galveston is the Port and Playground of the South, because of the shipping business the city enjoys and because it is a resort offering much to see and do for the entire family.

Many visitors come to Galveston to take advantage of the rich fishing grounds. Free and commercial fishing piers reach out into the waters of the Gulf; surf fishing is very big on the beach; those who prefer deep-sea fishing in the bay and out into the Gulf can join party fishing boats or charter private yachts or smaller craft. Fishing tackle can be rented, bait bought, and the necessary Texas fishing licenses purchased at bait stores, at the commercial piers, or in the county courthouse. (Offshore fishing does not require a license.)

The beaches of Galveston are equally attractive to visitors. All Texas beaches are free to the public. At both ends of the island cars may drive to the water's edge on the sand, though in other areas this is not permitted, in the interest of safety. Certain sections of the beach are designated surfing areas. Some of the beach is patrolled; other parts have lifeguards in attendance at certain times. Both free and paid parking is available. Steps from the top of the seawall down to the beach are strategically spaced along the entire length. It is possible to park free on the boulevard and walk down to the sand.

Exploring Galveston

To get the most out of your visit to Galveston, make your first stop at the Galveston Convention and Visitor's Bureau at 2106 Seawall Blvd. (east corner of the Moody Center facing the Marriott). You can stock up on maps and brochures. Specifically request *Galveston Island Attractions*. It is advisable that you have the brochure in advance. Toll free telephone numbers are 800–351–4236 in Texas, and 800–351–4237 outside the state. Also ask for the *Free Discount Coupon Book* offering reduced rates for accommodations, attractions and restaurants.

On the north side of the island, from 9th Street to 51st, is the harbor. To the east is the University of Texas Medical Branch, which incorporates, in just the few blocks between 4th and 13th Streets and the Strand and the post office (Avenue E), the University of Texas Medical School (1881; oldest in the state), John Sealy Hospital, the Shriners Burns Institute, Graves Psychiatric Hospital, Ziegler Tuberculosis Hospital, St. Mary's Hospital, the Child Care Center, the Marine Biomedical Institute, the Learning Center, and the Texas Department of Corrections Hospital.

Another orientation experience is the Treasure Island Tour Train. This is a pink, surrey-topped series of open cars pulled by their "en-

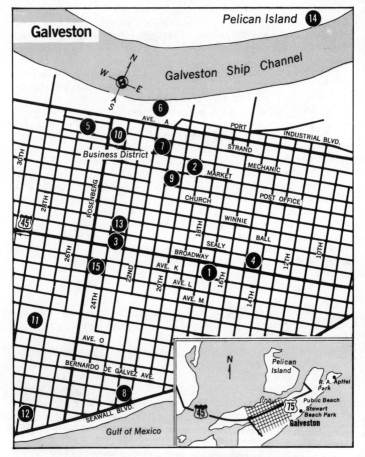

Points of Interest:

1) Antique Dollhouse Museum
2) American National Insurance Co. Tower
3) Ashton Villa
4) Bishop's Palace
5) Center for Transportation and Commerce
6) The Elissa
7) Galveston Arts Center
8) Galveston Convention and Visitors Bureau
9) Grand Opera House
10) Historic District
11) Kempner Park
12) Menard Park
13) Rosenberg Library
14) Seawolf Park
15) Sweeney-Royston House

gine" through both the old and the new parts of Galveston. The train goes through residential neighborhoods, where several historical homes are pointed out, passes the "Mosquito Fleet" at Pier 19, where an inner harbor is home for more than a hundred small fishing boats and shrimp trawlers, then wends its way to the Galveston Yacht Basin, where pleasure craft from all over the state are moored.

One other sightseeing trip will not only show the city, but provide transportation: "The Galveston Flyer," a motorized replica of an old-fashioned trolley, runs frequently and will allow you to get off and on at specific stops.

Another great attraction to Galveston is its large collection of restored nineteenth-century homes. Walk or drive through the Historic District. Maps and a tour cassette are provided by the Galveston Historical Foundation at the Visitor's Center, 2016 Strand; 765-7834.

Ashton Villa, the Bishop's Palace, and the Samuel May Williams house are open to the public daily. Some of the other restored houses are on view at special times during the year. For more details see the *Practical Information* section on *Historic Sites and Houses,* below.

The Strand and Seawall Boulevard

The Strand, once known as the Wall Street of the South when Galveston was the largest and most important city in Texas, has been revived and restored. The iron-front buildings have been repainted and refurbished. The old stores and warehouses are now occupied by cultural and business establishments. Most are open seven days a week, offering marvelous opportunities to eat, browse, and buy.

At the foot of the Strand, at 25th Street, is the Center of Transportation and Commerce, a railroad museum at Shearn Moody Plaza, in the old Santa Fe train station. No expense has been spared to make this railroad museum one of the finest in the country.

Galveston's 1877 "tall ship," *The Elissa,* at Pier 22, is within walking distance of the Strand. A children's playground with its own miniature tall ship adjoins that museum. Tours include a film of the restoration project.

Seawall Boulevard is the avenue that fronts the Gulf of Mexico. On the south side is the seawall; on the north, between 4th Street in the east end and 95th Street in the west, are most of the hotels, motels, and condos in Galveston.

Along the north, or land, side of Seawall Boulevard are many restaurants, souvenir shops, and establishments where you can rent skates, surfboards, pedal surreys, and bikes by the hour or the day.

Activities and Amusements

The entire island is geared for family fun and entertainment. Stewart Beach Park, on the east beach at the foot of Broadway Boulevard, has a complete bathhouse, various rides, arcades, two water slides, and a miniature golf course.

Sea-Arama Marineworld is located at 91st Street and Seawall Boulevard. This is an entertainment complex not only for children. It features professional sea- and land-animal shows, water revues, and fine aquatic displays. To "do" Sea-Arama properly should take about three hours.

Entertainment is year-round in Galveston. During the summer the historical drama *The Lone Star,* by Paul Green, alternates with Broadway favorites at the Mary Moody Northen Amphitheater at Galveston Island State Park, FM 3005 at the 13-Mile Road. The Strand Street Theater, Galveston's only repertory theater, always has something on the boards. The Galveston Symphony Orchestra presents regular and pop concerts throughout the year. Dance programs and visiting artists also play Galveston. For times and places check with the Galveston Convention and Visitors Bureau, in the Moody Civic Center at 21st and Seawall Boulevard, where most convention activities are held; 763–4311.

Take a free ferry ride. The Texas Department of Highways and Public Transportation provides free ferry service between Galveston and Point Bolivar. The ferry connects with Highway 87 on the Bolivar Peninsula of the Texas mainland. The round trip should take about forty minutes. On summer weekends expect a 2 to 3 hour wait to board in your car. A more practical idea would be to park your car on the Galveston side, in the lot near the ferry landing, then walk aboard. Another opportunity to cruise around Galveston Bay is aboard a Victorian-style paddlewheelboat. Not only can you see the city from the sea, but you can enjoy dinner and jazz cruises or romantic dance trips. Call 763–4666 for prices and times. Docked at Pier 22.

Galveston offers something for everyone, from birdwatching and bowling to zooming down water slides. Rent a sailboat or motor craft, or water ski from Washington Park at 61st and Offats Bayou, where the boat launch is. Tennis and golf packages are offered by several of the hotels and motels. Ride a horse, or fish, or walk along the top of the seawall or on the sand down at the water's edge. Or just lie in the sun.

PRACTICAL INFORMATION
FOR GALVESTON

 HOW TO GET THERE. There are three ways to get to Galveston Island: two by land and one by sea.

By car or bus from Houston, Galveston is a 50-mi. drive on Interstate 45, over the double causeway into the heart of the city. At the western tip of the island a toll bridge spans San Luis Pass. This is for traffic to and from the southwestern Gulf coast.

Highway 87 crosses East Galveston Bay. This route from Port Arthur and the northeast-Texas mainland requires transport by a ferry operated by the Texas highway department between Point Bolivar and Galveston Island.

The driving times to Galveston from other cities, in hours, are: Corpus Christi 4; Houston 1; Dallas 6; San Antonio 5.

Bus. Texas Busline, 765–7731, operates service between Galveston and Houston.

Cruise ship. Several cruise lines use the port annually between mid-December and the end of April. Check with your travel agent.

Airport limousine. The Galveston Limousine Service runs shuttle vans between Galveston and Hobby Airport and Houston Intercontinental Airport approximately every hour and a half. The schedules and rates are listed in the clearly designated waiting areas at both airports. The time between destinations can range from one to two hours.

Galveston has no train service and plane service comes and goes. Ask your travel agent to check.

 TELEPHONES. The area code for Galveston is 409. You do not need to dial the area code if it is the same as the one from which you are dialing. However, it will be necessary to dial "1" first if you are dialing outside the city to the other 409 areas. Information for Galveston is 1411; information for outside the city is 1–555–1212. An operator will assist you on person-to-person, credit-card, and collect calls if you dial "0" first. If you are seeking information for a toll-free "800" number, dial 1–800–555–1212.

 HOTELS AND MOTELS. There are many hotels, motels, and condominium suites to accommodate the tourists, but none can offer more than in-house swimming pools and temporary permission to play golf at the country club. Mobile-home parks and campgrounds are situated at both the east end and the west end of the island.

Hotel rates are based on double occupancy, European Plan (no meals). Categories, determined by price, are: *Expensive,* to $150; *Moderate,* $40 to $85; *Inexpensive,* $18 to $35. Most of the hotels are on Seawall Boulevard.

Flagship Hotel. 2501 Seawall Blvd.; 762–8681. On the beach side of the boulevard, the hotel is built on a steel pier that extends out over the Gulf of Mexico. Every room has a view of the sea and the city from its own balcony. Full-service facilities. The view is worth the stay. *Expensive.*

Marriott Hotel Galvez. 2024 Seawall Blvd.; 765–7721. A white, wedding-cake-type structure originally built in 1910. It faces the Gulf—as do most of its rooms—and is conveniently situated across from the Moody Civic Center. Full hotel services. No charge for children under 12 in the same room. Rates vary, depending on the time of year. *Expensive.*

The San Luis on Galveston Isle. 53rd and Seawall Blvd. 244 deluxe rooms, all with balconies overlooking the Gulf. Three restaurants, family plans available. *Expensive.*

Tremont House, 2300 Ship's Mechanic Row (one block off the historic Strand). 125 deluxe rooms and suites. Elegant. *Expensive.*

Hotel chains are represented by the following:

Airport Resort Inn, nr. Galveston Municipal Airport.

Best Western, 600 Strand, near the hospital.

Econo Lodge, 61st near the Blvd.

Gaido's Motor Inn, 3800 Seawall Blvd.

Holiday Inn, on the beach at 50th and Seawall Blvd.

Key Largo, 54th and Seawall Blvd.

Motel 6, 74th and Broadway on I-45 north side.

La Quinta Motor Inn, 1402 Seawall Blvd.

Ramada Inn, 50th and Seawall.

Republic Inn, 61st and I-45 on south side.

There are many other motels. For extensive information ask the Visitor's Bureau at 21st and Seawall Blvd., 763–4311, for their brochure listing accommodations and prices. Reservations are recommended during the summer. In the winter many of the hotels and motels have rooms from $20 to $40. Vacation packages are offered year-round.

For longer stays and larger accommodations, several condominiums rent their rooms and suites by the day, by the week, and for even longer.

By the Sea, 7310 Seawall Blvd.; **Casa del Mar Hotel Condominiums,** 6102 Seawall Blvd; **Islander East Condominium,** off Seawall Blvd. on the east end of the island, on the sand at 415 East Beach Drive; **Victoria Condotel,** 6300 Seawall Blvd.; **The Galvestonian Condominium,** 1401 East Beach Blvd.; **Seascape Condominium,** 10811 San Luis Pass Rd.; **The Reef,** 8502 Seawall.

On the other hand, if you would like to rent a house by the week or month, **Jamacia Beach,** 737–1044, **Pirates Beach** and **Pirates Cove,** 737–2771, and **Sand 'N Sea Properties,** 737–2556 and **Sea Isle,** 737–2750, all at the west end of Galveston, have such available.

Galveston now has nine bed-and-breakfast homes, or inns. Ask the Convention and Visitor's bureau for its "Accommodations" brochure, or call 762–0854, the bureau's central information number.

GETTING AROUND. The city bus system is not satisfactory for tourist destinations; a car is a necessity to get around Galveston. If you did not bring your own car, rental cars are available. See the Yellow Pages for offices and phone numbers. Taxis are plentiful; check the Yellow Pages and call for pickup. A shuttle trolley between the beach and the Strand will be ready by late 88.

TOURIST INFORMATION. The *Galveston Convention and Visitors Bureau,* 21st and Seawall Blvd. (763–4311), is in the Moody Civic Center building, the site of most conventions and many civic and social events. It is open daily in the summer but closes on Sunday the rest of the year. It has a collection of free brochures, booklets, pamphlets, and listings of the sightseeing opportunities in Galveston. Of special interest is *Galveston Island Attractions,* which lists almost everything available to the visitor, and "Galveston Island Accommodations," in which the locations and rates are cited.

The *Strand Visitors Center,* 2016 Strand (765–7834), run by the Galveston Historical Foundation, is open seven days a week from 10:00 A.M. to 5:00 P.M. It has a fine collection of free information especially relating to the projects of the Foundation. Audio walking tours by portable cassette recorder of the Strand and of the Historical District are available. The center has a 24-page activity and guide book for children entitled *Strand Discovery Tour,* for $2. A 10-minute orientation film, which plays continuously, will help you asess your sightseeing priorities. The Strand Visitor's Center also offers international Ticketron service. Always ask about Senior Citizen's rates.

Galveston Chamber of Commerce, 315 Tremont (23d St.; 763–5326), will also answer inquiries.

RECOMMENDED READING. Ray Miller's *Galveston; Bob's Reader* (Bob Nesbitt, 2608 Ave. O, Galveston, 77550). Both books are available at the Historical Foundation, Dicken's Bookshop on the Strand, and the Ashton Villa.

The Children's *Strand Discovery Tour* is now available at the Strand Visitors Center, 2016 Strand (765–7834) for $2. This 24-page activity book offers youngsters a fun-filled, easy-to-follow exploration of the Strand, the wharves, and the downtown area. Actually, no family should be without it. See the free film *Galveston—The Golden Age of the Gilded Isle* by Robert Cozens.

TOURS. The *Treasure Island Tour Train* departs from 21st and Seawall Blvd. alongside the visitors' bureau at specified hours during the year. Call 765–9564 or 744–1826 for schedules. Five trips go daily during the summer and two a day the rest of the year. The tours are of 1½ hour's duration, with commentary, passing through 17 mi. of old and new Galveston. The "train" consists of open cars, pink no less, with a fringe on top; 64 passengers can be accommodated.

The train rides along Seawall Blvd., passing the remains of Fort Crockett, which lived through two wars—though no shots were ever fired at it or from it in anger. It glides through typical neighborhoods, the historical district, the downtown business section, the Strand, and into the medical complex. (The University of Texas Medical Branch occupies more than 80 acres and comprises 53 buildings.)

It would be a good idea to take this tour before you begin sightseeing on your own; it will give you a clear idea of where everything is. Adults: $3.50; children 3 to 12: $1.75; kiddies 2 and under: free.

The Galveston Flyer, a trolley (really a bus designed to look like a trolley), leaves from 21st St. and Seawall Blvd., on the hour, from 9:00 A.M. to 5:00 P.M. daily. It makes stops at Ashton Villa at 24th and Broadway, at the Center for Transportation and Commerce, the railroad museum at 25th and Strand, continues down Strand to the visitors' center at 2016 Strand, remains on Strand to the east end, returns to Seawall Blvd., and makes the Galvez Hotel the last stop before beginning the run over again. Cost is $4 for adults; $3 for children; $3.50 for senior citizens. You may get on and off at your convenience at no additional charge. The tour is narrated.

Sightseeing Galveston Island by sea is also possible. *The Colonel,* a 150-foot-long paddlewheeler does tri-daily, narrated historical tours of the Galveston Bay harbor area. Adults: $8; children 4–12: $4. Evening: seafood dinner and jazz cruises. Adults: $24; children under 12: $15.00. Only on Friday and Saturday night does the *Colonel* do moonlight cruises on the Bay. This journey is for adults only, and sails from 10 P.M. to midnight; the cost is only $15.00. She is docked at the 22nd street wharf, a short distance from the Strand. Call 763–4666 for reservations and sailing times.

Tours in Other Areas. A worthwhile off-the-island trip is a visit to NASA, 30 mi. northwest on I–45 at the Johnson Space Center in Clear Lake City, on NASA Rd. 1. It is open to the public from 9:00 A.M. to 4:00 P.M. daily. Guided tours are available if you make previous reservations; (713) 483–4321. Ask at the visitors center information desk for self-guided tour maps.

The *Lunar and Planetary Institute* is also in this area, at 3303 NASA Road One. Advance tour arrangements are necessary. Call 486–2180 between 8:30 A.M. and 5:15 P.M. weekdays. Drive west on I–45 to NASA Road One; take the off ramp, turn right, and stay on that road until you come to the space center. Direction signs abound.

SEASONAL EVENTS. Special events come and go without notice sometimes. Check with the Strand Visitor's Center and the Convention and Visitor's Bureau for the latest information, and read *The Island of Galveston's TRAVELHOST,* a complimentary magazine to be found in your hotel, condo, inn, or B&B.

On the first and second weekends in May, the *Historic Homes Tours* are conducted. This is a project of the Galveston Historical Foundation. The tour features private homes that are not otherwise open to the public.

Mardi Gras is celebrated with parades and festivities during the week preceding Ash Wednesday.

The *Dickens Evening on the Strand* is really a weekend. During those two days on the first weekend in December the Strand re-creates an authentic Victorian holiday street scene. This outstanding winter event is sponsored by the Galveston Historical Foundation. Call 765–7834.

An annual *Easter Egg Hunt* and *July 4th picnic* are held at Ashton Villa on the appropriate days.

PARKS. At the eastern end of Seawall Blvd., down the ramp and on the sand, is *Apffel Park,* on Boddecker Dr. The park has boat-launching facilities, jetty and surf fishing, bait camps, restaurants, a recreation pavillion with concessions and gift shops.

Stewart Beach Park, 4th St. on the sand, has a complete bathhouse, an amusement park with rides, a skating rink, a miniature golf course, and water slides. See the *Children's Activities* section, below, for hours and prices.

Menard Park, between 28th and 27th Sts. and Ave. Q and Seawall Blvd., a small, block-square park, has a recreation building with restrooms, a large picnic area, and five concrete tennis courts—which are free; just come out and wait your turn.

Sea-Arama Marineworld is a unique family-entertainment complex featuring professional shows and attractions. Free parking. See *Children's Activities,* below, for details.

Galveston County Beach Pocket Park #1 is at 7½ Mile Rd. on FM 3005. This has picnic areas, playgrounds for children, showers, restrooms, and a boardwalk to the beach. Parking is $2.

Two miles west, at 9½ Mile Rd., is *Galveston County Beach Pocket Park #2,* and at the 11-mile road is park #3. Same facilities as Park #1. Parking at #2 and #3: $3.

Farther west, at 13 Mile Rd., is *Galveston Island State Park.* This beautiful 2,000-acre tract stretches from the Gulf to the bay. Ideal for birdwatching, it features nature trails. It has both day and overnight facilities. Hookups for trailers and RVs are available.

Seawolf Park on Pelican Island (cross the bridge at 51st) features picnicking, fishing facilities, and two World War II vessels to visit. See *Children's Activities,* below, for times and charges.

Two other quiet, cool areas are *Central Park,* a block-square area in front of the county courthouse at 21st and Winnie (Ave. G), offering nothing but a moment's respite between sightseeing sprints; and, at 27th and Ave. O, the *Garten Verein,* where a 12-sided Victorian building will catch your eye. The building is not open to the public except for special occasions.

CAMPING. *Galveston Island State Park* is on 13 Mile Rd., 6 mi. southwest of the Galveston city seawall, on FM 3005. This 2,000-acre park spans the width of the island from the Gulf to the bay. Recreational and natural features of the park include swimming, fishing, beachcombing, birdwatching, and nature trails along the 1.6 mi. of sandy beach—as well as camping.

Camping: 150 sites with water and electrical hookups; each has a shade shelter, picnic table, and cooking grill; restroom and shower nearby. $11 a night.

Screened shelters: 10 shelters, 9 by 12 ft.; electrical outlet; light and picnic table inside; water and cooking grill outside. $14 a night.

There is a group trailer area of 20 sites, with water and electrical hookups; restroom and showers nearby. $11 a night.

There are also picnic sites with shade shelters, picnic tables, and cooking grills, with a restroom and showers nearby. No reservations needed, and no charge for this amenity other than the entrance fee of $2 per day per vehicle that applies unless the visitor has an annual or restricted annual entrance permit or a parklands passport.

If you plan to stay, reservations will be accepted up to 90 days in advance for the overnight sites if you call (409) 737–1222 between 8:00 A.M. and 5:00 P.M. or write to the park at Rt. 1, Box 156A, Galveston, TX 77551.

Mobile-Home Parks are: Gulf View Trailer Park, 5800 Seawall Blvd.; 744–3382; Dellanera R.V. Park, FM 3005; 763–4311; and Bayou Haven, 6310 Heards La., off 61st St.; 744–2837.

Camping overnight on the sand beaches is permitted only in specified areas. Safety is the concern here. At the extreme end of West Beach is a licensed campground. Trailers and recreational vehicles are also welcome there.

BEACHES. State law forbids Texas beaches to be closed to the public. All 32 mi. of Galveston Island's beachfront is open. At certain times of the year automobile traffic is not allowed on the sand in specific areas, in the spirit of safety. There are many free places to park within a short walking distance to the water and many commercially-operated beach parks that charge for parking and amenities. The farther west one drives the less crowded the beaches become.

Commercially-operated beach parking areas provide various degrees of concessions, beach-apparatus rentals, bathhouses, sanitary facilities, and security. The Galveston County Sheriff's Department provides lifeguard protection in designated areas. Signs clearly indicate where surfing is permitted. The Galveston Park Board of Trustees, is responsible for the cleanup of the public beaches; a $200 fine for littering is enforced.

Across Seawall Blvd. from each hotel are stairs leading down to the sands. Again, this is not a private beach. It is a convenience for the guests at the hotels who don't want to drive to the beach. A car is necessary to reach the beaches not at your doorstep, since city public transportation is not scheduled for tourists.

PARTICIPANT SPORTS. There is a wide range of activities open to those who wish to take part in the action. Seawall Blvd., which extends to over 10 mi. of continuous sidewalk—the longest in the world—presents an ideal **walking, jogging, skating, and bikeriding** expanse. Single- and 10-speed bikes, as well as surrey-type pedal vehicles, are available for rental at numerous locations along the boulevard between 6th and 20th Sts. At Beach Bike Rental the surreys cost $7 an hour.

Surfing is permitted along specifically designated areas of the beach. Several spots on the beachfront rent surfing equipment by the hour or by the day.

Water-skiing lessons are given at Washington Park, near the boat launch, on Offats Bayou and 61st St.

Horses to be ridden along the beach can be rented at the Sandy Hoof Stables, 11118 W. Beach, between 7 and 8 Mile Rds. off FM3005; and the Gulf Stream Stables at the 8 Mile Road and West Beach.

Tennis. Menard Park, between 27th and 28th Sts. and Ave. Q and Seawall Blvd., has five free concrete courts. The Galveston Racquet Club, 83rd and Airport, 744–3651, charges nonmembers for instruction and use of the courts.

Golf. Galveston has two 18-hole courses. Pirates Golf Course, 1700 Syndor Lane, west on Stewart Rd., is a public course. The Galveston Country Club, 9 mi. farther west on Stewart Rd., 737–1776, is private but extends reciprocal privileges if you belong to another golf club or if you are staying at a hotel or condominium that offers golf packages.

FISHING. Galveston Island is famous for its fishing opportunities, and no wonder. More than 52 varieties of fish swim in the temperate waters on and surrounding Galveston Island. Angle from free and commercial piers, wade into the surf, drop a line in the inlets and bays, join a party fishing-boat excursion for bay and deep-sea action, or charter your own small craft for more privacy.

If you opt for fishing from the piers that extend into the Gulf, you will find free piers on the seawall at 10th, 17th, 27th, 29th and 61st. Sts. The rock groin jetties at the entrance to the harbor at the east end of the island, and at Washington Park on Offats Bayou at 61st St., are also free.

The commercial piers are beyond the Flagship Hotel at Seawall Blvd. and 25th, at 91st St., and at Seawolf Park on Pelican Island. Well-stocked bait-and-tackle shops, at which refreshments can also be bought, will be found on the commercial piers, where the cost to fish is $2.50 for adults and $1.00 for children. If you rent a rod it will be another $3.00, and you'll have to leave a $10.00 deposit. Bait is $2.50 to $3.00. These piers are open 24 hours. A state fishing license is required for those aged 17 to 65. Licenses may be bought at any bait camp or sporting-goods store. Some convenience stores sell them, as does the Galveston County Courthouse. See the Yellow Pages under "fishing bait" to expedite matters.

Party boats provide the easiest way to do your deep-sea fishing. It is wise to make reservations as soon as you know when you intend to go. These boats go into the bay or the Gulf. They have all the necessary equipment designed to make your day a success; all the tackle and bait are provided, sonar locates the fish, and the crew is helpful and courteous. (Anti-seasickness pills are recommended for Gulf trips.) The trips are usually of 12-hour duration, departing about 8:00 A.M. Rates are $43 on weekdays and $53 weekends and costs $11 a person for 4-hour bay-fishing excursions. All these boats belong to Galveston Party Boats, Inc., at Pier 18; 763–5423.

Texsun II (762–8088) has private boats for charter, at Pier 19. Blue Water Charters at the Galveston Yacht Basin (762–5365) and Reel Fun Charters at 400 Strand (762–3319) do too.

You will find more boat charterers in the Yellow Pages, and the Convention Bureau's pamphlet entitled *Galveston Island Attractions.*

Seawolf Park on Pelican Island charges $2 to fish from the pier. The Galveston Island State Park at 13 Mile Rd. west on the island includes fishing privileges in the daily $2-a-car fee.

 CHILDREN'S ACTIVITIES. Galveston has developed its well-earned reputation as a family resort with several installations that will keep the children occupied and delighted for hours.

Sea-Arama Marineworld, 91st and Seawall Boulevard, 744–4501, is open daily at 10:00 A.M. All the shows and attractions operate every day until dark. To see the several live shows and all the exhibits and displays should take about three hours. There is a snack bar on the ground level, and other opportunities to buy ice cream or cold drinks in other spaces. Don't miss the great performing dolphin shows and sea lion shows. Exotic birds and snakes also perform. A water-ski show and more than 20 Killers of the Deep should not be missed. Adults: $7.95–$4.95 for children 4 to 12. The entire family will enjoy this unique educational-entertainment complex. Parking free.

Seawolf Park on Pelican Island, 744–5738, is on the site of what once served as the quarantine station through which all immigrants passed as they came into the port of Galveston. Today a three-level pavilion offers a magnificent view of the harbor. Tables and chairs are strategically placed for dining and picnicking convenience. To the east is the *Selma,* a World War I concrete ship that went aground and sank. Many fishermen drop their lines off this ship. At the pavilion snack bar, hot food and cold drinks can be bought for a picnic overlooking the harbor, where small sailboats and huge cargo vessels glide by. A 380-ft. fishing pier enables the anglers to bring in flounder and trout while the children cavort in the imaginative playground. Two vessels are on exhibit: the U.S.S. *Cavalla*, one of World War II's most distinguished submarines, and the U.S.S. *Stewart*, a World War II destroyer. The park is open dawn to dusk. Prices are $2 for parking; $2 for the tour of both ships. To get to Seawolf Park take Broadway (Avenue J and also I–45) to 51st St. Turn north, cross the bridge, and continue straight down the main road until you reach the park, about 10 min. from 51st.

Stewart Beach Park, at the foot of Broadway on the sand in the east end of Galveston, 765–5023, is the most developed of several municipal beach parks.

Parking during the week, Monday through Friday, from 8:00 A.M. until 6:00 P.M., and on Saturdays and Sundays from 6:30 A.M. to 8:00 P.M., costs $3 per car, truck, or van. The closing date for the park is October 31 each year; it opens again on February 16—though the beach itself is accessible year-round.

The bathhouse facilities' hours are the same as above, and are free. A locker, good all day, is 50 cents.

Connected with Stewart Beach are *Sky Rapids*, 762–1993, open from 10:00 A.M. until dark, daily.

Bumper Boats and the *Roller Skate Track* are open 10:00 A.M. to 7:00 P.M. during the week and 10:00 A.M. to 10:00 P.M. on weekends.

The *Go Carts*, open 9:00 A.M. to dark daily.

The Peter Pan Golf Course, which is open from 8:00 A.M. until there are no more customers, 762–6619.

There are snack bars selling food and cold drinks. The beach is near for swimming. Chairs and umbrellas are for rent at the water's edge. Lifeguards are on duty.

West End Attractions—which means beyond 61st St.—include (at press-time):

Jungle Surf, 92nd and Seawall Boulevard. Open from 10 A.M. to dusk.

The *Sandy Hoof Stables,* 11118 West Beach, 740–3481, is open 8:00 A.M. until 6:00 P.M. You can hire a horse and ride along the beach, $10 an hour. Phone first.

HISTORIC SITES. Downtown adjacent to the harbor is the *Strand*. The section of the Strand along the equivalent of Ave. B, from 20th to 25th Sts., was once known as the Wall Street of the Southwest. It was Galveston's financial center in the last century, and in this neighborhood big business flourished in shipping, insurance, and banking. Today the Strand contains one of the finest concentrations of nineteenth-century iron-front commercial buildings in the United States. It has been designated a national historic landmark, and many medallions of the Texas Historical Commission can be seen on both sides of the street.

The Strand is being returned to its former glories. The nineteenth-century iron-front buildings have been painted and restored; once-empty stores now house eating places, boutiques, businesses, night spots, art galleries, artisans' studios, and an old-fashioned candy factory. The area between 20th and 25th is lighted as it was before the 1900 storm (a time from which almost everything in Galveston is dated)—by gas. For further information call at the Strand Visitors Center at 2016 Strand, 765–7834, or write to the Galveston Historical Foundation, P.O. Drawer 539, Galveston, TX 77553.

Also downtown, three blocks north of The Strand, is the 1894 *Grand Opera House* at 2020 Postoffice (Ave. F). During its era, "The Grand" was known as the Palace of the Southwest, presenting outstanding performances in drama, opera, music, and dance. Celebrities such as Sarah Bernhardt, Lillian Russell, Anna Pavlova and the czar's Imperial Russian Ballet, William Jennings Bryan, Otis Skinner, and John Philip Sousa and his band graced that stage. Galveston was not only one of the busiest ports in the nation, but a cultural center as well.

The theater became a cinema, saw hard times, and eventually closed its doors. Now the Grand has been acquired by the Galveston County Cultural Arts Council and has been restored to its former magnificence. The Grand is a functioning concert hall, fully heated and air-conditioned. It is home to Galveston Arts' nine-month-long Performing Arts Series, featuring symphonies, operas, ballets, and more, as well as concerts by touring troupes and local companies such as the Galveston Symphony. Rock, country-and-western, and bluegrass musicians also appear onstage, particularly during the summer. For information call Galveston Arts at 763–6459.

Worth a visit too is *St. Joseph's Church,* 2206 Avenue K. It is a simple frame structure with a rich Victorian Gothic interior. It was built by German immigrants in 1859. The church has been restored and is being developed into an ecumenical museum to display the city's religious history. The GHF has tour information; 765–7834.

HISTORIC HOMES

The citizens of Galveston are aware that their city has more than 500 structures of historical significance. In fact, Galveston is reputed to have more nineteenth-century homes in good condition than any other city in the country. Many of these sturdy houses have been restored to their former splendor and are private residences, but some are open to visitors.

One of the most elegant is *Ashton Villa,* 2328 Broadway (762–3933). Built in Italianate style before "the war" (in this case the Civil War), this three-story mansion is surrounded by spacious lawns and towering shade trees. The house is made of bricks fired on the island, and it is completely furnished and restored to its antebellum beauty. Tours begin in the restored carriage house with a multimedia presentation, *The 1900 Storm.* This 12-min. documentary tells of Galveston before the turn of the century, the unpredicted 1900 hurricane, its impact on the island, and the remarkable recovery by Galvestonians. Well-informed volunteer docents take visitors through the house, recounting the history of the lives led there. Children of all ages love the miniature dollhouse. Times: weekdays, 10:00 A.M. to 3:30 P.M.; weekends, noon to 5:00 P.M.; closed Tuesdays, September to May. Admission charged.

The Bishop's Palace, 1402 Broadway (762–2475), was officially opened on January 1, 1893. It was designed by Galveston architect Nicholas Clayton and took seven years to build. During the 1900 storm this limestone-and-granite house provided shelter for hundreds of homeless victims. The owners built this lavish mansion with an eye to entertaining. It is said that they had as many as 1,000 guests at a time. In 1933 the house was sold to the Catholic diocese, the present owners, as a residence for the bishop, though it was rarely used for that purpose. It is open to the public from noon until 4:00 P.M. daily. There is an admission charge: $3 for adults, $1.50 for children. This house is the most widely known architectural attraction in Galveston, and it is ranked among the top 100 homes in the United States for architectural significance.

A block west of Ashton Villa, at 2428 Broadway, is the castle-like building known as *Open Gates.* The 1889 home of the George Sealys was designed by Stanford White and made of Belgian half-brick in Roman style. The house is now owned by the University of Texas Medical Branch and is being restored for use as a conference center, and is not open to the public.

Yet another area of preservation of 40 blocks of Galveston's beautiful residential historical sector reaches from Broadway to Market and from 11th to 19th Sts. Structures within this East End Historical District cannot be changed without consent of a city board. This district has been designated a national historic landmark and is listed on the National Register of Historic Places. A map depicting this area can be picked up at the Strand Visitors Center at 2016 Strand. This will help you with a self-guided tour by car, bicycle, or foot. A cassette tape is also available.

Three other houses are worth a visit:

The *Samuel May Williams Home,* 3601 Ave. P (or Galvez), is one of the oldest buildings on the island. It was a prefab, built in Maine and shipped to Galveston in 1839. It is now restored, even to the authentic furnishings, and is open to the public. The Galveston Historical Foundation will give times; 765–7834. Admission: $2.50, adults; $2, senior citizens; $1.25, students and military.

J.R. Smith House. 2217 Broadway (765–5121). Open for daily tours. Also offers six elegantly furnished guest rooms for B&B.

The *Syndor-Powhatan House,* 3427 Avenue O (763–9374), is the headquarters for the Galveston Garden Club. It was built in 1847, is completely restored and furnished; open for tours weekends. Call first. Admission charged.

 MUSEUMS. When we speak of museums in Galveston we do not mean giant ethnic, anthropological, or astronomic enterprises. The historic homes and the restored Strand area, which are designated as national historic landmarks, are living museums, and some are open to the public. Galveston has several other installations that serve as museums. Although the time spent within their confines has a cultural aspect, "entertaining" and "fun" might be more descriptive of your visit to any or all of them.

Antique Automobile Museum. 23rd and Ave. M; 765–5801. Open daily 10 A.M.–5 P.M. This is a marvelous collection. The kids will like it, too. $4, adults; $2.50, children. $10 for the entire family.

The Center for Transportation and Commerce. This is a first-rate five-acre museum at the foot of historic Strand and Rosenberg (25th) Sts., in the Shearn Moody Plaza. The museum was completed in mid-1982. It took four years and $5.5 million to create this, one of the finest, most unusual museums in the world.

A parking lot at the museum's front door (behind the main building) accommodates 200 cars. The entrance is into and through an 1875 depot, complete with telegrapher's table, ticket window, pot-bellied stove, and the sounds heard in train stations of that era. Innovative audio-visual techniques present the history of Galveston, from those days in the early 1500s when the Karankawa Indians began to trade with the islanders to what the city is today. A working HO-gauge miniature railroad is the heart of an exhibit of the activities of the port of Galveston. The focal point of the museum is the People's Gallery, "A Moment Frozen in Time—1932" in the original train-station waiting room. This gallery consists of 39 life-sized models in monochromatic white plaster, all in positions of motion and all authentically attired. Outside on the four once actively used train tracks is a collection of 35 railcars, four steam locomotives, baggage and boxcars, a Pullman, a parlor car, a caboose, and the *Anacapa*, a deluxe 1929 private railcar. Adults, $4; children, $2. Open daily all year. Call 765–5700 for information.

The Elissa. A towering survivor of the Age of Sail, this ship is ranked as Texas' number-one tall ship. The *Elissa* is berthed at Pier 22 adjacent to the Strand. A film, public tours, and exhibits tell her story. The *Elissa* is the oldest ship in Lloyds Register of Shipping and is the third-oldest merchant ship afloat. This 430-ton, 160-ft., square-rigged sailing ship was built in Scotland in 1877. In 1883 she brought cargo into the port of Galveston. She has sea-traded around the world and changed hands and names several times, once even becoming a smuggler's vessel. In 1975 the Galveston Historical Foundation bought her, and completely restored her to be fully operational. Tickets may be purchased at Pier 22, or at the Strand Visitors Center, 2016 Strand; 765–7834. $3.50, adults; $2.50, children.

The Rosenberg Library. The first library in the state—and one of the finest—is at 823 Tremont (23d St.) (763–8854). It contains artifacts and pictures of early Galveston and Texas history. The library has an extensive collection of rare books and documents. The several art galleries within the building have continually changing exhibits. It has a vast collection of large-type books. Open Monday through Saturday.

Galveston County Historical Museum. Newly opened. 2219 Market St. (766–2340). Offers a variety of programs and exhibits. Free.

Remember to ask about senior-citizen rates at all the above listings where a fee is charged. Frequently such information is not volunteered. This also holds true for many hotels and restaurants.

THE ARTS, THEATER, MOVIES. *The 1894 Grand Opera House,* 2020 Postoffice, has been restored. The resurrection of this theater, which once presented the top stars from around the world, is the site for solo entertainment, group concerts, and presentations of drama and the dance. For information on events, and self-guided tours, call 763–6459.

Beach Band Concerts. Weekly during the summer months, at the Gazebo behind Ashton Villa at 24th and Ave. I.

The Strand Street Theatre, 2317 Mechanic (Ave. C), is Galveston's only professional repertory company. Presentations include musicals, drama, comedy, and classical works. For information on current show and prices, call 763–4591.

Galveston Arts Center, 202 Kempner (22d St.); 763–2403. Scheduled exhibits, classes in dance, theater, music, creative writing, ceramics, pottery, painting, weaving, drawing, printmaking, photography, and filmmaking. Usually fully booked. Some classes are single presentations; others are done in a series.

The Galveston Symphony Orchestra. Now in its sixth year, it is composed of local talent, with the conductor from the Houston Symphony Orchestra. The orchestra presents several fine symphony concerts and some pops concerts each season. Check the local paper for programming.

The *Mary Moody Northen Amphitheater.* In the Galveston Island State Park, 12 mi. west of the city; 737–3442. The Lone Star Historical Drama Association presents two smashing outdoor musicals from late June through August. *The Lone Star,* a historical drama, and Broadway musicals—*Hello Dolly* this season —alternate. Performances are at 8:30 P.M. Go early to the Amphitheater Chuckwagon Restaurant, open 5 to 8 P.M., for barbecue before the show. A souvenir shop is also open.

Movie theaters. Galvez Mall, 61st and Broadway (I–45), has Cinema I, II, and III.

 SHOPPING. Galveston's downtown has gone the way of similar areas in many other cities. Besides the Strand, there is little other than banks and a few stores. Victoria Market, a remodeled business building on Postoffice (Ave. E) at 22d St., has a few boutiques.

On the Strand between 20th and 25th Sts. are boutiques, eating places, jewelers, craft shops, and art galleries.

To the east end of Galveston, on the Strand from 4th to 6th Sts., is the Port Holiday Mall, a shopping center across from the Best Western Galveston Resort and the University of Texas Medical Branch. The Fair, a branch of a chain of Texas specialty shops, is the anchor, and a supermarket, a restaurant, and several small stores occupy the lower level. All air-conditioned. Free parking.

At the west end of Galveston, 6402 Broadway (Ave. J, also I–45), is another covered, air-conditioned shopping center known as the Galvez Mall. This is the largest mall in Galveston and offers total shopping. Two large department stores which anchor each end of this mall belong to Sears on the east and Eibands to the west. Between them can be found specialty stores selling all kinds of merchandise. A hairdresser, three cinemas, and several eating opportunities are among the many businesses and boutiques here.

King Saver supermarket and Eckerd (general merchandise and drugs) hold down a two-block row of stores at Ave. S between 59th and 61st Sts.

Along the beachfront, on Seawall Blvd., extending from 6th to 91st Sts., are souvenir shops that sell T-shirts, bathing suits, sunning lotions, caps, visors sun hats, shells straw items, and everything typically found at resorts to tempt the tourist. Two piers, which extend over the beach and Gulf waters at 2201 and 2215 Seawall Blvd., have a complete stock of such merchandise.

In the Strand area you will find stores selling a great selection of merchandise. The Old Strand Emporium, 2112 Strand (763–9445), open seven days a week, 10:00 A.M. to 6:00 P.M., is a delicatessen, sandwich shop, and gourmet grocery with a wine cellar. They sell coffee beans and will custom grind them to your order. Go for lunch; stay to shop. La King's Confectionary, 2323 Strand, is an old-fashioned candy store that makes its own merchandise, and you can watch them do it. There is also an old-fashioned soda fountain where banana splits of days of yore, and Cokes flavored with your favorite taste, can brighten your life. They also serve sandwiches. Tuesday through Saturday, 10:00 A.M. to 6:00 P.M.; Sunday, 1:30 to 6:00 P.M. Another Galveston "must."

 DINING OUT. Galveston is famous for its seafood—not surprising, considering that it is an island in the Gulf of Mexico. Some of the restaurants featuring fish are diversified enough to have meat and fowl on the menus. Some are known for their methods of preparation: fried, broiled, grilled, sautéed, smothered in fancy sauces, or boiled and served cold. Galveston offers a large selection of restaurants for the most discerning palates.

Because Galveston is a resort that also caters to quick eaters on holiday, the fast-food franchises are well represented on all the main thoroughfares: Broadway (I–45), Seawall Blvd., 61st St. between Broadway and the Boulevard—and there is a cluster off 61st St. and Ave. S (Stewart Rd.). These are all inexpensive.

The price classifications and abbreviations below are based on an average three-course dinner for one person for food alone; beverages, tax, and tip would be extra. *Inexpensive* means less than $7; *Moderate* means between $10 and $20; *Expensive* is up to $25 and more.

Credit cards are usually accepted. Visa and MasterCard are the most popular, but if you have another one, ask. Travelers checks are not too welcome but may possibly be cashed. Out-of-town personal checks will do only if you have a major credit card.

Most of the restaurants listed here are open for lunch and dinner even if they close early. It is a good idea to check times, since they alter with the seasons.

We have not listed every restaurant in every category. The listings below are just a selection of places enjoyed by the locals. The Visitors Bureau at 21st and Seawall Blvd. has a list of other dining opportunities, as do the Yellow Pages, which are more extensive.

CONTINENTAL

Clary's. 8509 Teichman Rd., 740–0771. *Expensive.* West end; (Across from Galveston News Building. West on Broadway [I–45], off at 83d, under the freeway and right on Teichman's Rd.). Noted for seafood prepared in a variety of ways; steaks are top quality. If you don't like heavy seasoning, say so when you order. Make reservations if you don't want to stand in line. All credit cards.

The Wentletrap. 2301 Strand, downtown in the historical district; 765–5545. *Expensive.* This restaurant has a long and varied menu and an even longer wine list. Specialties of the house often depend on the fish caught in island waters that day. The meats are top grade (delicious and tender), and the chef is justly proud of his sauces and seafood concoctions. The restaurant is in the 1871 T. J. League Building, which has been handsomely restored to create a relaxed ambience and Old World elegance. Open seven days a week for lunch, cocktails, and dinner. Reservations are recommended for dinner. So are coat and tie. All credit cards.

Café Torrefie. 2126 Strand, downtown; 763–9088. *Moderate.* Not usually as expensive as The Wentletrap—but it can be. This restaurant is in a restored bank building. In fact, for special occasions, dine in the old vault. Relaxed ambience. Reservations are recommended. All credit cards.

The Merchant Prince in the Tremont House is noted for its nouvelle cuisine. *Very expensive.* Reservations not necessary. All credit cards.

SEAFOOD

Gaido's. 3818 Seawall Blvd., on the beachfront; 762–0115. *Moderate to Expensive.* Gaido's has the reputation for the finest stuffed flounder ever prepared by human hands. Everything prepared to your special order. MC, V.

Hills Pier 19. 20th and Wharf; 763–7087. Downtown, a block north of the Strand, on Galveston Bay. *Moderate to Expensive.* The food is acquired cafeteria-style, but the location is what counts. Above the restaurant, on two broad open decks, are tables where one can dine after selecting the food, which is prepared right before your eyes. Watch the fishing boats and shrimp trawlers come home at twilight, or the big cargo vessels and tankers on their way out of the port. This is the most exciting view in town. The food is good but may be expensive, though there are inexpensive lunch specials. Seven days a week, 11:00 A.M. to 7:00 P.M.

Shrimp & Stuff #1. 3901 Ave. O; 763–2805. An informal and *inexpensive* place to take the kiddies. Nothing elegant, but the food is tastefully prepared and not greasy. **Shrimp & Stuff #2,** 68th and Stewart Rd., west of 61st St., is also *inexpensive* and a family-style operation. They have also expanded to hamburgers, roasts, and chicken.

ETHNIC RESTAURANTS

Mario's Flying Pizza. 2202 61st Street; 744–2973. *Moderate.* Italian. Makes the best Fettucini Alfredo this side of the Atlantic. And their pizzas and other pastas are also superb. Family style; closed Mondays.

Tong's Happy Buddha. 2827 61st St.; 744–5774. Chinese food, well prepared and pleasantly served. A family restaurant. Lunch is *inexpensive;* dinner is *moderate.*

Corella's Corral. 2528 61st street, west end; 744–9138. *Inexpensive.* The Mexican meals here are not too highly seasoned, although the staff will supply you with the hot stuff if you prefer that spicy taste. Family style. Monday through Saturday, 10:00 A.M. to 8:45 P.M.

MISCELLANEOUS

Dinner on the Diner. Set in a vintage dining car within the Railroad Museum at 25th and Strand. *Expensive.* Call 763–4759 for reservations.

Le Marche. Sandwiches, light menu, bakery, in Eiband's Department Store in the Galvez Mall at 61st St. on the north side of Broadway (I–45). *Inexpensive.*

Primo's. 7711 Broadway. From "Tex-Mex" to Bar BQ. *Moderate.* Call 744–1617 for directions.

The Warehouse. 101 14th St., east end, one block north of the Strand; 765–9995. *Inexpensive.* Typical Texas barbecue of ribs or chicken; huge hamburgers, and always fresh French fries. 10:00 A.M. to 8:00 P.M.

HOTEL DINING ROOMS

Marriott's Hotel Galvez, the *Flagship, La Quinta,* the *San Luis,* the *Tremont House,* both *Holiday Inn,* and *Gaido's Motor Inn,* along with many of the other motels, have coffee shops and/or gourmet dining rooms. The prices range from expensive to moderate and, in some cases, inexpensive, depending on where you are and what you order.

 NIGHTLIFE. Galveston—so far as nightlife is concerned—is no Paris or Manhattan, or Houston for that matter. If you do feel the need to get out on the streets at night, there are plenty of bars, lounges, beer parlors, and nightclubs here. However, their popularity shifts rapidly, and by the time you read this book, many of the places listed would be out of business or might have moved—so we won't try to list them now.

The best bet for the visitor is to try word-of-mouth recommendations at the time of the visit. Another good idea would be to stick to the hotel and motel lounges, which remain pretty stable; popular night spots include the bar at the restored Marriott's Hotel Galvez, 21st and Seawall Blvd., and the *Lookout Lounge* at the Flagship Hotel, Rosenberg (25th St.) and Seawall Blvd. Both feature live popular music for dancing. *Hemmingway's,* in the Key Largo Motel at 5400 Boulevard (744–5000), has live music as does the San Luis. The Tremont House has a pianist nightly in the lobby-lounge.

The *Wentletrap Restaurant,* 2301 Strand (see *Dining Out*), has a jazz pianist evenings, and *Café Torrefie,* 2126 Strand (see *Dining Out*), features a variety of musical offerings from jazz to folk to modern country.

Index

FODOR'S TRAVEL GUIDES

Here is a complete list of Fodor's Travel Guides, available in current editions; most are also available in a British edition published by Hodder & Stoughton.

AVAILABLE AT YOUR LOCAL BOOKSTORE OR WRITE TO
FODOR'S TRAVEL PUBLICATIONS, INC., 201 EAST 50th STREET, NEW YORK, NY 10022.